BELIEVING
GOD
DAY BY DAY

BETH MOORE

BELIEVING GOD

DAY BY DAY

DAY BY DAY

GROWING YOUR FAITH
ALL YEAR LONG

B&H
PUBLISHING GROUP

NASHVILLE, TENNESSEE

ISBN 978-0-8054-4798-9
B&H Publishing Group
Nashville, Tennessee
www.BHPublishingGroup.com

Dewey Decimal Classification: 234.2
Faith \ God–Promises

Printed in China
1 2 3 4 5   12 11 10 09 08

DEDICATION

To my beloved church family at Houston's First Baptist Church—I am nearly overcome with emotion as I attempt to find words to express my gratitude and love for you. You have been everything that constitutes a true church "home" to me for more than twenty years. You have loved and supported me and given me a safe place to make mistakes so I could grow. You have been my constant during a time of such change in my ministry life. A place of normalcy and stability, you have been my harbor.

With deepest affection I dedicate this particular book to you because you are a church that has an undeniable history of believing God. We have seen some miracles together, haven't we? Not bad for a bunch of Baptists. God is good . . . and patient. I wouldn't trade you for the world. Thanks for everything.

"You are My witnesses"—the LORD's declaration—"and My servant whom I have chosen, so that you may know and believe Me and understand that I am He."

Isaiah 43:10

INTRODUCTION

God thrust the Sword of the Spirit in my feeble hands some twenty years ago when He sent me into a young adult Sunday school class as the teacher. Apply that last word loosely. Actually, I was an idiot.

I got a brand new Bible for the journey and I meant to keep it that way. I neglected it. Fumbled it. Dropped it. Opened it. Yawned over it. Whined over it. Cried over it. Begged God to help me with it.

Then slowly but surely, one discovery at a time, I fell head over heels in love with it and with its brilliant Author. I dug my fingernails into it and vowed never to let go. I may have a whole junkyard of broken vows somewhere but, to the glory of God, that one is not in the heap.

While strengthening my grip on the Sword of the Spirit, God began wedging the Shield of Faith in my other hand so that I'd learn to use them the way He intended: in tandem. Mind you, I thought I had plenty of faith. After all, how much faith does a church-going, church-serving soul need?

I would soon learn the answer: a whole lot more than I had. As forcefully as God has ever spoken to my heart, He said, "You believe *in* Me, Beth. Now I want you to believe Me." The words "believe Me" arose out of Isaiah 43:10 like a dead man leaping to his feet. "You are my witnesses," declares the LORD, "and my servant whom I have chosen, so that you may know and believe me" (NIV).

Believe me. Believe me. BELIEVE ME. Those two words have echoed unceasingly in my mind ever since.

For reasons known only to a forgiving God, I've spilled quarts of ink through books and Bible studies in attempts to share a passion to love God and know Him. I will continue to express these holy obsessions in one way or another as long as God wills. The book you hold in your hand is my attempt to articulate my own personal journey toward obedience in believing God, while encouraging you to join me in the blessed experience.

I am convinced that Christ is always the initiator of matters concerning faith. So if I'm on target, you've neither stumbled onto this book nor accidentally found it in your hands. Christ is initiating a fresh anointing of faith in your life, Dear One. He wants to put a fresh belief in our systems! We have been assigned to this world during vital days on the kingdom calendar. Yet too often we have dropped our shield, making us more vulnerable to defeat. God is calling His church to draw the Sword of the Spirit (the Word of God) and lift high the Shield of Faith.

Do it, Dear One. No more business as usual. From here to eternity, stay a verb and wake a few nouns. Live by faith. Live out loud. And never stop believing God—day by day.

With much love,
Beth

JANUARY

In every situation take the
shield of faith . . . and the sword
of the Spirit, which is God's word.
Ephesians 6:16–17

This book is about developing an action verb faith. It's about getting out there where we can feel the wind of God's Spirit blowing in our faces. It's about learning that we don't have to put down the Sword of the Spirit (the Word of God) to raise up the Shield of Faith.

The way I see it, that's why God gave us two hands. If we want to live abundantly, we must pick up both. To pick up the Sword of the Spirit without the Shield of Faith is to shrivel and dry up in the desert of legalism. To pick up the Shield of Faith without the Sword of the Spirit is to try walking on quicksand.

This book of instruction must not
depart from your mouth . . . for then you will
prosper and succeed in whatever you do.

Joshua 1:8

Is it working? Your belief system? Is it really working? God's intention all along has been for His children to succeed. So I ask you, is your Christian life feeling successful? Are you achieving and experiencing what Scripture says you would?

God stated unapologetically that conditions exist under which "you will prosper and succeed in whatever you do." But the only way we are going to impact our generation is to prove that our faith in Christ is real and that it works.

For countless Christians, I'm convinced it's real. My concern is whether or not we have the fruit to suggest it works.

Watch out, brothers, so that there won't be
in any of you an evil, unbelieving heart that
departs from the living God.
Hebrews 3:12

Why isn't our present practice of Christianity working? Why don't we see more
of God's promises fulfilled?

It's the same reason why the practices
of the Israelites in the wilderness didn't
work and why they never reached the
land they'd been promised. Like them,
we can be dramatically delivered from
bondage, leave our Egypts, and yet never
make it to our Promised Lands. We, too,
can find ourselves lodged in a desolate
wilderness between the two. Scripture
supplies the one-word explanation: "So
we see that they were unable to enter because of unbelief" (Heb. 3:19).

The doubter is like the surging sea, driven
and tossed by the wind. That person should
not expect to receive anything from the Lord.

James 1:6–7

Firsts have great importance in Scripture.
Do you know the first recorded words
that ever came from the serpent's mouth?
"Did God really say . . ." (Gen. 3:1). He
used the spade of deceit to sow doubt.

Satan, posing as the serpent, couldn't
keep Eve from believing in God, so he
did the next best thing. He baited her,
tempting Eve not to believe God or trust
His motives. Her walk was crippled, her
doubt was contagious, and the couple
lost the land that God had placed under
their feet. When Eve dropped her shield
of faith, every other piece of her spiritual
armor became vulnerable.

He did not commit sin, and no deceit was found in His mouth.... [He] committed Himself to the One who judges justly.

1 Peter 2:22–23

Over and over in Scripture, when God was about to move in the lives of His people or instruct them to reposition themselves, He began with a reminder of who He was. A thumbs-up of sorts.

God knew that the most powerful driving force the children of Israel would have—the power that would press them toward their earthly destiny—was their certainty that the One who went before them was who He said He was.

It's true: God is who He says He is. In fact, He is either everything He says He is or He's a liar—unworthy of any faith at all.

Lord, I have heard the report about You;
Lord, I stand in awe of Your deeds.
Revive Your work in these years.

Habakkuk 3:2

I'm convinced that most of us more readily accept the fact that God is who He says He is than we believe He can do what He says He can do. We less quickly assume that God is able—or perhaps more pointedly, that He is willing—to do what He says.

Ironically, however, God can do what He says He can do precisely because He is who He says He is. His many titles describe His ability. As Savior, He saves; as Deliverer, He delivers; as Redeemer, He redeems; as Master, He assumes authority; as Bread of Life, He provides; and as Almighty, He exerts divine strength.

Not to us, LORD, not to us, but to Your name
give glory because of Your faithful love,
because of Your truth.

Psalm 115:1

I want my children to love God. I want
them to love His Word and discover the
life, healing, and power within it. I want
them to love people and treat them with
compassion and kindness.

But more than anything on earth—
tears fill my eyes as I write this—I want
glory to come to God through them.

I want a thousand things for my children, and I ask without hesitation, but I
want nothing more than that God would
be glorified. Life is just a breath. All that
will matter forever in our heavenly state
is the glory that came to God through
their lives and ours.

The one who draws near to Him
must believe that He exists and
rewards those who seek Him.
Hebrews 11:6

I am who God says I am. This truth un-
earths emotion in me every time I say it
because I am reminded of the journey
I've had to take to believe it. More than
any other faith challenge I face, believing
that I am who God says I am necessitates
choosing what God says over what I feel.

I want so much to be a woman of
faith. In fact, I'd give just about anything
to be a woman God would characterize
by her faith, since nothing pleases Him
more (Heb. 11:6). But if I'm really serious
about believing God, I also have to believe what God says about me. No small
challenge. How about you?

Whether well-fed or hungry, whether in abundance or in need . . . I am able to do all things through Him who strengthens me.
Philippians 4:12–13

You really can do it, you know. Whatever the harrowing path that's before you, you really can walk it victoriously. God will give you every place you step your feet for the glory of His name if you let Him.

How do I know this? For starters, the verse above claims that a servant of God can do all things—*all* things—through Christ who gives him strength.

This "all things" includes even those things that are otherwise impossible. And it leads us to a statement of faith that isn't just a cheer or a feel-good memory verse. It is sound theology yearning to become our reality.

I will shake the house of Israel among all
the nations, as one shakes a sieve, but not a
pebble will fall to the ground.

Amos 9:9

The first ten years I spent in the Word, I
believed that every doctrinal view I held
was absolutely right and all others were
unquestionably wrong. I was an aerobics
teacher at our church gym, for crying out
loud. I worked out all morning and stud-
ied Scripture all afternoon.

But one way God widened my world
was by pitching me out of the gym and
into the heat of a spiritual war. I spent the
next several years in intensive care with
God as He began rebuilding me from the
inside out so I could teach harder lessons
but with a softer spirit. Don't be surprised if He does the same for you.

The word of God is living and effective and sharper than any two-edged sword.... It is a judge of the ideas and thoughts of the heart.

Hebrews 4:12

Sometimes I actually feel the Holy Spirit within me quickening to the Word of God as I study it, mix it with faith, and pray to absorb it. But even when I don't feel anything, I count on supernatural fireworks within.

See, God says His Word is alive and powerful, and I believe Him. He also says His Word is powerful when it's in me. Yes, me—a bundle of faults, fears, and insecurities. Just think! My weakness is not strong enough to wound God's Word. Neither is yours. God does His job. He speaks to accomplish. We don't have to make Him. We just need to let Him.

From the fruit of his mouth
a man's stomach is satisfied; he is filled
with the product of his lips.

Proverbs 18:20

Mankind possesses complete uniqueness among all creatures because we are created in the image of God. Our unique ability to communicate through words is one of the most obvious evidences of the image we bear.

The element of divine communication being transmitted to the inhabitants of the earth is so critical, so paramount, that Christ Himself is called the Word that "became flesh and took up residence among us" (John 1:14). And by virtue of our creation in His image, our words—like His—possess an element of accomplishing and achieving power.

"We can't go up against the people because they are stronger than we are!" So they gave a negative report to the Israelites.

Numbers 13:31–32

A vital part of learning the *walk* of faith in our journey to and through the Promised Land is learning the *talk* of faith. The account in Numbers 13–14 of the Israelite spies being sent to explore the land clearly reveals the power of words.

Not only did the bad report of a few turn into the grumbling of the masses, it also led to vain imaginations. By the time the faithless words rolled around in their heads a while, the men had already pictured themselves dead and their wives and children taken as plunder. It's true that our minds feed our mouths, but our mouths also feed our minds.

... so that you won't become lazy,
but imitators of those who inherit the
promises through faith and perseverance.
Hebrews 6:12

The middle of any challenging journey can be the most critical point. Many of us may not be where we were, but we're not yet where we want to go. Perhaps the terrible bondage of Egypt is behind us, but the land of promise seems remote.

The longer we wander in the wilderness between Egypt and the Promised Land, the greater the chance that we'll return to captivity. The pull of familiar comforts and habits can feel overpowering, particularly against the uncertainty of Canaan's unknowns. But as we persevere, God is faithful to continually give us the extra push of motivation to press on.

Be transformed by the renewing of your
mind, so that you may discern what is the
good, pleasing, and perfect will of God.

Romans 12:2

Every believer needs the hope of second
chances. Some of us need lots of them.
God is fully aware of this. He looks upon
our hearts and knows whether we have
any authentic desire to be different or if
we're all talk.

And when lasting change finally does
come, few things are as healing as the evidence that the cycle is breaking. We may
have the same old struggles, but we're
making some new decisions. We know
we're coming full circle with God when
we stand at a similar crossroad where we
made such a mess of life before, but this
time we take a different road.

"Remove the sandals from your feet, for the
place where you are standing is holy."
And Joshua did so.

Joshua 5:15

God promises to always be with us, but
every now and then He reveals His presence a little more vividly than we were
expecting. That's exactly what God did
with Joshua just outside Jericho, when
"the commander of the LORD's army" appeared, audibly speaking to him.

God determined that if His servant
was going to step into a holy moment,
he'd better do it with bare feet. "And
Joshua did so." If I could get a clue about
the greatness of God, I'd be mortified by
all the times He told me to do something
and the record showed, "Beth did not do
so." Help me, Lord.

May you be strengthened with all power,
according to His glorious might, for all
endurance and patience, with joy.

Colossians 1:11

You've probably noticed that what God requires from us to live in victory can differ greatly from season to season. In some seasons, for example, He demands everything we've got—times when we feel like our life depends on it, times when we can't even think about tomorrow because we don't know how on earth we're going to live through today.

I'd like to suggest that some of the most adventurous endeavors you'll have with God may be too difficult at the time to enjoy. And by the time the party comes, you may smell too bad to go. Ah, but after a shower and good look back . . .

In Christ Jesus neither circumcision nor uncircumcision accomplishes anything; what matters is faith working through love.

Galatians 5:6

Faith is God's favorite invitation to make the impossible possible. He is greatly glorified when we are each enabled to do what we're unable to do. And I can think of few things further beyond our capabilities than loving those we don't want to love and loving those we don't even like.

But if we will place 2 Corinthians 5:7 (which tells us to live by faith) next to the verse above from Galatians 5, I believe we can come up with two life challenges that, if accepted, catapult us onto a path infinitely higher than this world's self-centered interstate of mediocrity: "We live by faith. We love by faith."

My Father is glorified by this:
that you produce much fruit and
prove to be My disciples.
John 15:8

Certainly those of us who have accepted Christ as our Savior have received the automatic and glorious result of eternal salvation. However, the primary reason why God left us on earth after our salvation was for our Christianity to "succeed" right here on this turf.

Sure, we're getting by, but getting by was never our destiny. We were meant to be profoundly effective. Why have we accepted average? Are the few effects most of us see and experience all that Christianity has to offer, all we can expect? If so, someone needs to feel sorry for us. I'd volunteer, except that I no longer buy it.

The report of your
obedience has reached everyone.
Therefore I rejoice over you.

Romans 16:19

God's willingness and unwavering desire to bless His people is one of the most repetitive concepts in both testaments of His Word. He is the Giver of all good gifts and greatly exults when a child cooperates enough to receive some.

Just as the Promised Land was a place of assured blessing to the children of God who followed His precepts in the Old Testament, New Testament believers were also promised blessing for their obedience. When you and I find our places in Christ where God can freely fulfill His promises to us, we too will experience immeasurable blessing.

With whom was He "provoked for 40 years"? Was it not with those who sinned, whose bodies fell in the desert?

Hebrews 3:17

You and I can be safely tucked in the family of God and have the full assurance of a heavenly inheritance without ever occupying the land of God's fulfilled promises on earth. Like the children of Israel, our carcasses can fall in the wilderness.

Traveling in Africa, my husband and I once came upon the sight of a cow's entire carcass polished to the bone by a lion. It reminded me how many times Satan— that "roaring lion"—had tried to destroy my life, witness, and fruitfulness. Will we let him have the satisfaction of cleaning our carcasses because we let them drop in a desert of defeat? God forbid.

This is why you must take up
the full armor of God, so that you may
be able to resist in the evil day.
Ephesians 6:13

Just like the children of Israel, we will always have an enemy that wants to keep us out of our Promised Lands. If we're going to win our battles, however, we need to wise up to some of Satan's schemes and prepare in advance for victory.

Our warfare is complicated by opposition that is much harder to identify than Hittites, Perizzites, and Amorites. In Ephesians 6:12, Paul tells us that "our battle is not against flesh and blood, but against the rulers, against the authorities, against the world powers of this darkness, against the spiritual forces of evil in the heavens." This requires the full armor.

Acknowledge that the LORD
is God. He made us, and we are His—
His people, the sheep of His pasture.
Psalm 100:3

You and I have got to know, not just
hope or think, that the One who cut covenant with us through the torn flesh of
Jesus Christ—Elohiym, the God over all
creation—is the same One who sits upon
the universe's throne, having spoken the
worlds into existence.

Surrounded by a society that spouts
many gods but at best nobly agrees to
equate them, you and I can know that the
Lord is God. Hoping we're on the right
track will never dig a deep enough path
to follow to our Promised Lands. We're
not going anywhere of profound eternal
significance until we know.

I am doing a work in your days,
a work that you will never believe,
even if someone were to explain it to you.

Acts 13:41

Before God insisted on calling me to fresh faith several years ago, I certainly believed He was who He said He was, but I was much less sure that He still works miracles in our day. I had been taught that God does not work many miracles today because we live in a different time period on the kingdom calendar.

Not only did God prove me wrong, I think He had a fairly good time turning my neatly compartmentalized belief system upside down. He seems to like saying, "Oh, yes I will" to the "Oh, no He won'ts," proving His own people wrong to prove His Word right.

He fell facedown and prayed, "My Father!
If it is possible, let this cup pass from Me.
Yet not as I will, but as You will."
Matthew 26:39

God and I have this deal. I know He has endless resources and that I will never ask more than He can supply, so I feel free to ask for anything I desire, then I try to jump up and down with a grateful heart for all He grants.

At the same time, God knows my absolute priorities—my A list of prayer requests. Therefore, if something on my A list temporarily or even permanently (ouch!) might have to cancel out something on my B list, so be it. I'll bend the knee, however painfully, because I am most desperate to know and experience the truest of all riches.

Moses asked God, "Who am I that
I should go to Pharaoh and that I should
bring the Israelites out of Egypt?"
Exodus 3:11

Let's just say I haven't been a low mainte-
nance project for God. I have definitely
been the problem. Goodness knows, God
has done His part. I once told my staff
with much laughter that if I die suddenly,
my gravestone might appropriately offer
this insight into my departure: "God got
tired." I just require lots of work.

That's why I have a little hang-up
saying that I am who God says I am. I
tend to want to rewrite it: "I *strive* to be
who God says I am." But that's not what
the Word says. Nope, it says I am already
who God says I am. If you have received
Jesus as your Savior, so are you.

We observed His glory, the glory as the
One and Only Son from the Father,
full of grace and truth.

John 1:14

No matter how mighty the servants of
God like Moses and Joshua were, the
"One and Only" shoes tend to run large
and slap around awkwardly on a walk. But
when Christ came to earth, He stepped
His feet into those "One and Only" shoes
and, for the first time in all of human history, they were a perfect fit.

Wriggle your bare toes and celebrate
that He's been wearing them ever since.
No need to try them on. His plan hence-
forth was not to use just one person but
many: a corporate body of believers for
each generation, each bringing their gifts
to the mix. He's the only One and Only.

So faith comes from what is heard,
and what is heard comes through
the message about Christ.

Romans 10:17

I grow more convinced all the time that an ongoing relationship with God through His Word is essential to the Christian's consistent victory. We can't presently and actively believe God in our day-to-day challenges if we are not presently and actively in His Word.

For example, God's direction for my life will escape me without the Word being "a lamp for my feet and a light on my path" (Ps. 119:105). Liberty in Christ only becomes a reality in life through knowing and applying the truth of God's Word, not just taking our Bibles to church or keeping them on our nightstands.

Life and death are in the
power of the tongue, and those
who love it will eat its fruit.
Proverbs 18:21

With the exception of kings, judges, and
dictators, the application of the above
verse from Proverbs is primarily figurative. But make no mistake: it is far from
diminutive.

We possess no small power in our
tongues. Most of us can testify that the
human tongue owns the power to kill all
sorts of things. Relationships, lifelong
dreams, and self-confidence are only a
few of the common fatalities. Thankfully,
however, perhaps as many of us have also
experienced life-giving words of encouragement, instruction, and exhortation.
We need His Word on our lips.

For by your words you will
be acquitted, and by your words
you will be condemned.
Matthew 12:37

If you and I want to abide and flourish in our Promised Lands, we're going to have to get rid of some bad reporting, faithless talking, and negative grumbling. Words wield power. Our words are not omnipotent, but they are still potent.

We can tear down with our words or build up with our words. We can speak living words, or we can speak killing words. We can encourage, or we can discourage. The question is not whether our words affect; the question is how. Even if you're a quiet person, you still communicate often through words, and just as often through affecting words.

As soon as . . . their feet touched the water
at its edge, the water flowing downstream
stood still, rising up in a mass.

Joshua 3:15–16

Every now and then a friend teases me
about being a drama queen. I don't deny
it, but I also don't mind saying that God
is the ultimate drama King. He didn't
have to make biblical scenes exciting,
like this miraculous crossing of the Jordan River in Joshua's day. He could have
achieved His will just as completely by
compulsory, methodical order.

I'd like to suggest that God Himself
enjoys the drama. Everything about the
Israelites' Promised Land adventure was
electrifying, even when it was terrifying.
Yours is liable to be similar. God's path-
ways to promise are anything but boring.

FEBRUARY

It has been given to you on
Christ's behalf not only to believe in
Him, but also to suffer for Him.
Philippians 1:29

Have you lived much of your life in a repetitive cycle? Ultimately, how the cycle
continues is based on one of two things:
prevailing belief or prevailing unbelief.

Keith and I often say that we failed
and flopped our way to faith, but somehow through the grace of God, we kept
falling forward. As long as we wear these
cumbersome suits of flesh, we are not going to be supermen flying high in the sky
of faith. We are called to something far
more elementary: to walk by faith. God
most often looks for what prevails in our
lives. If unbelief prevails, we find ourselves repeating cycles of defeat.

After the seventh time, the priests blew
the trumpets, and Joshua said to the people,
"Shout! For the Lord has given you the city."
Joshua 6:16

The number seven in Scripture is believed by many scholars to be the number
of completion. The creation seems to be
the paradigm. The seven days and seven
repetitions God required of the Israelites
before He'd give them Jericho was a literal time frame for them, but it presents
a figurative application for us.

During certain stretches of life, God
requires us to follow a fair amount of repetition for a considerable amount of time
until He deems a season complete. Then
all of a sudden He seems to do something
profound or miraculous, and we can't fig-
ure out what changed.

Jacob, why do you say, and Israel, why do you
assert: "My way is hidden from the LORD,
and my claim is ignored by my God"?
Isaiah 40:27

I wonder if you've ever fought a fiercely
demanding battle you didn't cause. An
illness? A layoff? The untimely death
of a loved one? A house fire? Suddenly
worthless stocks?

Any number of situations can arise
that you or I didn't directly cause, yet
we're thrown into long-term overdrive
to deal with them.

It's true that some of the most difficult and demanding seasons of our lives
will seem grossly unfair. But we can ex-
pend so much energy whining about the
unfairness of our situation that we have
nothing left to invest in the real fight.

We know that we have passed from death to
life because we love our brothers. The one
who does not love remains in death.

1 John 3:14

We may go on for years, expending untold hours of self-sacrifice (if not the rest
of our lives) trying to love certain people
in certain situations—all without seeing
any apparent fruit.

Yet God has called us to love even
when we don't want to, when we don't
feel like it, when we get nothing in return,
when they don't deserve it, when they're
not worth it, when they don't even know
it—when it makes no difference. If we're
not confronted by God to love someone
in this season of our lives who brings out
many of these same feelings in us, we're
probably not getting out enough.

Jesus said, "Because you have seen Me,
you have believed. Those who believe
without seeing are blessed."
John 20:29

The church, comprised of all believers in
Jesus Christ, is generally pretending she's
cloaked with kingdom power and effectiveness when in reality she has exposed
herself in powerlessness to the ridicule of
the world.

We can't blame the devil. It's just
that for the most part, we've dumbed-
down New Testament Christianity and
accepted our reality as theology rather
than biblical theology as our reality.
We've reversed the standard, walking by
sight and not by faith. We want to be the
best of what we see, but frankly what we
see is far removed from God's best.

None of the good promises the LORD
had made to the house of Israel failed.
Everything was fulfilled.

Joshua 21:45

I don't want to be counted among the
faithless who never claimed the land
God promised them. All that will matter
about our earthly lives when we receive
our heavenly inheritance is whether we
fulfilled our callings and allowed God to
fulfill His promises.

I know that I'm going to make it to
heaven because I've trusted Christ as my
Savior, but I want to make it to my Canaan on the way. I want to finish my race
in the Promised Land, not in the wilderness. You too? Then we need to cash in
our fear and complacency and spend all
we have on the only ticket out—*belief!*

We must be sober and put the armor
of faith and love on our chests, and put on
a helmet of the hope of salvation.

1 Thessalonians 5:8

Above all, you and I need to learn to take
up our shield of faith or we will fall. And
when we fall, we'll fall hard. I definitely
know the feeling. Don't you?

We also desperately need to know
the Word of God and to wield the Sword
of the Spirit so that when the enemy slyly
suggests, "Did God really say . . .?" as he
said to Eve, we can know the answer em-
phatically. When we respond to attacks
of doubt, distortion, and deceit with the
truth of God's Word, the fiery dart is ex-
tinguished and the enemy takes another
hit. Heaven knows I owe him a few. You
too? Then let's take our faith seriously.

The fool says in his heart,
"God does not exist." They are corrupt;
their actions are revolting.

Psalm 14:1

The opinions of our culture span the entire spectrum from the belief that God does not exist all the way to the belief that God is who an inspired text says He is. In my estimation, atheism demands far more faith than theism, so I have never been significantly tempted to disbelieve in the existence of God.

The evidence in His favor is simply overwhelming. I wouldn't have enough energy for the endless rationalizations demanded to explain existence without Him. Those who believe in a godless universe can't even find a beginning to base their belief system on.

Jesus Christ, who was preached among you by us . . . did not become "Yes and no.". . . For every one of God's promises is "Yes" in Him.

2 Corinthians 1:19–20

Christ gave His life so God could say yes to the fulfillment of His promises in the lives of believing mortals. Therefore I am utterly convinced that any "no" an earnestly seeking child of God receives from the Throne is for the sake of a greater "yes," whether the fulfillment is realized on earth or in heaven.

A present-active-participle believer in God will see miracles, all right. But note this: the greater miracle doesn't need to be spectacular to be just as certain and special—like abundant life, redemption, ministry, and exceeding harvest after a "no" we felt we wouldn't survive.

How much more will your
Father in heaven give good things
to those who ask Him!
Matthew 7:11

If we have priorities concerning what we believe to be the best that life has to offer our children, would we be surprised to think that God does too? Ours is a God of priorities. Might He have an A and a B list? I wouldn't be surprised if He has a list for each of us stretching all the way from *alpha* to *omega*.

After all, "How great is Your goodness that You have stored up for those who fear You" (Ps. 31:19). Scripture is replete with God's bountiful desires for us, but He also clearly knows what He desires most to accomplish, not only in each believer but in each generation.

These were the names of the men
Moses sent to scout out the land, and Moses
renamed Hoshea son of Nun, Joshua.

Numbers 13:16

We may not know exactly when Joshua received his new name from Moses, but we don't have to be biblical scholars to reason why he might have needed one. In essence, his original name Hoshea means "deliverer," while his new name Joshua (or Jehoshua) means "Jehovah delivers."

If I were flesh and blood chosen by God to lead a grasshopper people into a land of giant opposition, I'd want to know He was the true Deliverer, not me.

I'd like to suggest that Joshua not only needed to know who he was, he needed to know who he wasn't. He wasn't God. Not a bad lesson for any of us to learn.

On the contrary, all the more,
those parts of the body that seem
to be weaker are necessary.
1 Corinthians 12:22

Let's refute the mistaken mentality that God mightily uses a few chosen people in each generation to fulfill His kingdom agenda and that everyone else is basically insignificant. Under the inspiration of the Holy Spirit, Paul stressed the importance of the whole body of believers working together.

Simply put, Christ left us too much to do to leave it up to a few. You are an honored part of the body of Christ, and your contributions add up. Remember, God's New Testament math specializes in addition and multiplication, not subtraction and division.

Therefore, observe the words of this
covenant and follow them, so that you will
succeed in everything you do.
Deuteronomy 29:9

I've been saying it a lot in this book, but
only because it's of utmost importance:
We have to learn how to use the Word of
God if we want to be a powerful force for
the kingdom and against the darkness.
We'll never abide in our Promised Lands
unless God's promises abide in us.

God set the standard with Joshua
when He told him to keep the Word
continually on his tongue, meditate on it
day and night, and live by its commands.
"For then you will prosper and succeed
in whatever you do" (Josh. 1:8). With all
my heart I believe living on and by God's
Word is still the key to true success.

A man will be satisfied with good
by the words of his mouth, and the work
of a man's hands will reward him.
Proverbs 12:14

In both my junior and senior years, I was blessed to study high school English under a graciously demanding teacher. She was the first person who ever suggested that I had a writer buried somewhere within me.

I fell into much sin, hypocrisy, and despair after those days and was certain that whatever promise I may have possessed at one time, I probably forfeited to my foolishness. After many books and Bible studies, I still don't see myself as a writer, but every now and then I think, "Mrs. Fanett did." Never underestimate the power of words.

The message is very near you,
in your mouth and in your heart,
so that you may follow it.
Deuteronomy 30:14

You and I want to function in the full
throttle of power that God desires to
give us. And a significant portion of that
power involves our mouths. Ideally, our
faith can become voice, and our voice can
become the right kind of power, when
we're operating in the will of God.

Every conversation does not have to
be blatantly spiritual for God to make it
positively effectual. Sometimes God gives
us favor with people who are touched or
impressed with how we express ourselves
because God empowered our words even
though the listener couldn't distinguish
the difference.

Then they believed His promises and sang
His praise. They soon forgot His works and
would not wait for His counsel.
Psalm 106:12–13

God never forgets His promises to us. In
turn, He intends for us as His children
never to forget His faithfulness to fulfill
them—every single one of them.

Over and over in Scripture, God's
people are told to actively remember all
He has done on their behalf. In fact, the
practice of remembering is so important
to the children of God, He often diagnosed their seasons of rebellion as being
serious cases of forgetfulness.

One of the most powerful motivations for believing God in our present
is intentionally remembering how He's
worked in our past.

You delivered me from death,
even my feet from stumbling, to walk
before God in the light of life.
Psalm 56:13

Perhaps many of us have experienced a
deliverance of some kind. Certainly those
who are believers in Christ have been
delivered from a general and otherwise
hopeless bondage to sin. But Christians
can also unfortunately experience areas
of captivity long after conversion.

My personal history of deliverance
began when I accepted Christ as Savior.
But since that time, He has also delivered
me from tremendous insecurity, much
fear, very defeated thinking, and self-
destructive patterns of sin. You've likely
experienced deliverance of one kind or
another, too. Thank Him for that.

As for you, continue in what you have
learned and firmly believed, knowing
those from whom you learned.

2 Timothy 3:14

One of the most important messages to learn in your Christian life is that, yes, you can believe God for something dramatic and miraculous. But in between dramatic revelations, what's a believer to do? The day-in, day-out fundamentals, that's what.

Prayer. A daily time in God's Word. Praise and worship. Attending church. Serving a church body. Giving. These are the fundamentals, and they'll never change. We can make all the excuses in the world for not practicing this one or that, but they nonetheless represent the backbone of obedience.

Save me, God, for the water has risen
to my neck. I have sunk in deep mud,
and there is no footing.
Psalm 69:1–2

Have you ever had someone to blame, and that "someone" was *you?* Have you ever smacked yourself on the head for something stupid you've done? How often do we lose the battle to our own bitterness rather than to our opposition?

Make no mistake: Satan's specialty is psychological warfare. If he can turn us on God ("It's not fair!"), or turn us on others ("It's their fault!"), or turn us on ourselves ("I'm so stupid!"), we won't turn on him. If we keep fighting within ourselves and losing our own inner battles, we'll never have the strength to stand up and fight our true enemy.

Each person should examine his own
work . . . not in respect to someone else. For
each person will have to carry his own load.
Galatians 6:4–5

The very nature of love is sacrificial. In
fact, if we're not presently feeling the
squeeze and sacrifice of loving someone,
we're probably exercising a preferential,
highly selective, and self-centered human
substitute.

But mind you, loving another person sacrificially does not equal subjecting
ourselves to untold abuses. God doesn't
call us to sacrifice our sanity; He calls us
to sacrifice our selfishness. When those
lines are vague or unclear, I can give you
no more important advice than to seek
sound, godly counsel, just as I have done
before at various times.

He showed me the river of living water,
sparkling like crystal, flowing from the
throne of God and of the Lamb.
Revelation 22:1

I was taking my usual route on my morning walk when I happened upon a simple scene with telling application. Four
ducks were splashing in a mud puddle in
the sidewalk while a large, pristine pond
was just over a small hill.

I stopped in my tracks and stared,
as though God were saying to me, "Beth,
that's like my church, splashing in a mud
puddle with a sea of living waters within
her reach, just on the other side."

No one has been covered with more
mud from puddles-settled-for than I. If
God can move me from the puddle to the
pond, I assure you He can move you.

The Lord's message rang out from you, not
only in Macedonia and Achaia, but in every
place that your faith in God has gone out.
1 Thessalonians 1:8

The reason most of our present belief
systems aren't working is because they
are big on systems and small on belief.
What you and I need is a fresh belief in
our systems. Faith is the only thing that
will close the gap between our theology
and our reality.

We'd be hard pressed to find a more
consistent priority God places before
His people in either testament. Yes, love
is His greatest commandment, but any
of us who have accepted the mammoth
challenge of biblical love in difficult circumstances can testify how much faith
was required for obedience.

These will serve as tassels for you to look at,
so that you may remember all the LORD's
commands and obey them.
Numbers 15:39

I believe there are certain things we can
do that invite the pleasure and power of
God. I am by no means suggesting we
play "Let's Make a Deal" with God or try
manipulating Him for miracles. God is
not a paid performer and would not be
shy to show His disapproval over an inappropriate approach.

Let's be careful, though, that we don't
err in the opposite extreme of faithless
caution. A big difference exists between
trying to manipulate God to give us what
we want and cooperating with God so
He can give us what *He* wants. The latter
is our goal.

It would have been better for them not to
have known the way of righteousness than,
after knowing it, to turn back.

2 Peter 2:21

The most dangerously influential opinions are those held by intellectuals and
scholars who profess Christianity but
deny the veracity and the present power
of the Bible. The obvious brilliance of
these scholars supported by a convincing
list of degrees tempts those who want to
believe God's Word to feel gullible and
ignorant. The unspoken indictment is,
"How could you be stupid enough to believe that?"

Like Eve, we want to feel smart, so we
end up making the stupidest decision of
our lives. Nothing is more ignorant than
choosing man's intelligence over God's.

When He entered the house, the blind men
approached Him, and Jesus said to them,
"Do you believe that I can do this?"
Matthew 9:28

We can always hope and pray diligently
for a miracle. If in God's sovereignty He
chooses to accomplish His purposes another way, let it not be that we "have not"
because we "ask not" (James 4:2) or because we believe not.

If you dare to believe and yet don't
get your miracle, God has a greater one
planned. If what you desperately need or
deeply desire is founded in the Word of
God, don't let anyone tell you that God
can't or that He undoubtedly won't. Remove the wonders from God, and you
can no longer call Him wonderful. Has
He ceased to be wonderful to you?

As a result, they were all astounded
and gave glory to God, saying, "We have
never seen anything like this!"

Mark 2:12

With all my heart, I believe God is willing to perform outstanding miracles in our generation as we increase our faith. I have and will continue to ask God to perform wonders on behalf of my loved ones and those whom I serve.

At the same time, I also believe that the greatest miracle of all is glory coming to the Father through mortal creatures. If God can gain glory through the miracle I've requested, hallelujah! If I don't get my miracle but God gets greater glory, I believe I received the greater miracle with the most eternal dividends. We are most blessed when God is most glorified.

Why am I so depressed? Why this turmoil within me? Put your hope in God, for I will still praise Him, my Savior and my God.

Psalm 42:5

At times, the psalmist addressed his own soul as if to get through to his stubborn will. How often you and I could use this same approach! Speak these words from Ephesians 1:3–8 aloud to your own soul as many times as it takes to start believing them: "In love I am blessed, chosen, adopted, favored, redeemed, and forgiven."

Your soul is not the only one that needs to hear them. Keep these truths handy so that you can spit them at the accuser the next time he condemns you. He knows you'll be too handicapped to live in consistent victory until you believe who and what God says you are.

They conquered him by the
blood of the Lamb and by the
word of their testimony.
Revelation 12:11

I'm talking to you, not to your preacher
or your Bible study teacher. Your legacy
can still be having an impact in a dozen
generations if Christ tarries. You don't
have to look a certain way, receive a certain gift, attend a certain church, practice
a certain kind of ministry, or establish a
nonprofit organization.

All you need for being mighty in
your generation is faith and the Word of
God. Through Jesus Christ you can absolutely, unequivocally do anything God
places before you. This includes (among
other things) getting that stinkin' enemy
off your Promised Land!

You welcomed it not as a human message,
but as it truly is, the message of God, which
also works effectively in you believers.

1 Thessalonians 2:13

Unlike any other text, the Word of God
has supernatural effects for those who
receive it by faith. When we receive it by
reading it, meditating on it, believing it,
and applying it, the life of the Word becomes lively in us.

The power of God's Word becomes
powerful in us. The activity of the Word
becomes active in us. The operations of
the Word become operative in us. The
energy of the Word becomes energizing in us. The effectiveness of the Word
becomes effective in us. It invades every
part of our being, even the marrow of our
bones and the motives of our hearts.

MARCH

When we put bits into the
mouths of horses to make them obey us,
we also guide the whole animal.

James 3:3

A vital element in learning to walk by faith and obedience is learning to *talk* by faith and obedience. We might think of it like this: God's words are *omnipotent*. Our words are *potent*.

Both the Bible and our own personal experience teach us that human words possess a great deal of power. James 3:4 compares the tongue to a small rudder with the power to steer a large ship. James 3:6 compares the tongue to a fire that can corrupt and set aflame the whole person. Our words are potent no matter how we use them, but what would happen if we allowed God to take hold of them?

Your speech should always be gracious,
seasoned with salt, so that you may know
how you should answer each person.
Colossians 4:6

For months I had small-talked with a
beautiful Indian woman, a Muslim, who
works at my neighborhood dry clean-
ers. One day she leaned over the counter
with surprising warmth and asked, "Mrs.
Moore, what do you do for a living?" To
my delight, she was very touched when I
told her. I believe she wasn't turned off
because the timing was right.

God had intrigued this precious
woman through simple small talk and
graciously gave me favor with her. You
also have countless occasions for God to
turn what seems to be meaningless chat-
ter into powerful, affecting expression.

The God before whom my fathers Abraham
and Isaac walked, the God who has been my
shepherd all my life to this day.
Genesis 48:15

I have made a lot of memories with my
family—memories that seem engraved
on my mind forever. My relationship
with God, however, preceded my present family and proceeded long after my
mother died. In other words, my longest
and most effectual history with anyone
has been with God Himself.

So I have loved Him longer, known
Him better, and experienced life with
Him more intimately than with anyone
else. God and I have made some memories together. Hard ones. Good ones. Astounding ones. You don't have to know
God long to make memories with Him.

The LORD your God dried up the waters of
the Jordan before you . . . just as the LORD
your God did to the Red Sea.

Joshua 4:23

Yes, the Israelites had been in a situation
like this before. After observing their
first Passover, the Red Sea stood between
them and freedom. God parted those
waters and the people passed through on
dry ground, only to fall into a wilderness
drought of unbelief.

At the Jordan they received a do-
over—a new opportunity to walk through
parted waters. They could remain in the
wilderness or proceed to their Promised
Land by faith. Choosing to believe, they
made the right decision. The old cycle
was broken, and a new cycle ushered
them into their destiny—by faith.

He said to them, "If anyone wants
to be My follower, he must deny himself,
take up his cross, and follow Me."

Mark 8:34

Sometimes the greatest proof of God's miraculous power is when an attention-deficit seeker of instant gratification denies himself, takes up his cross, and follows Christ . . . for the long haul.

When we look back at our lives, our favorite parts are those stones of remembrance—major places where God did something big or where we acted in bold faith. But *God's* favorite parts are the lines in between where we chose to walk faithfully without answers and visible evidences. This is what fans the flame of God's desire to show us His glory. Faithfulness invests in the future.

The LORD threw them into
confusion before Israel. He defeated them
in a great slaughter at Gibeon.
Joshua 10:10

Dear One, God doesn't just want us to defend ourselves in fierce seasons of battle. He wants us to wound the kingdom of darkness.

I remember Keith and I watching one of the early *Rocky* sequels. We stared at the screen while Apollo Creed pummeled Rocky's poor face without getting a single return punch. Keith leaned over to me and said, "That's the old 'let 'em hit you in the face till they're tired' trick."

Some of us think that if we just stand there and let Satan hit us long enough, he'll get tired. He's not getting tired! Hit him back, for crying out loud!

Above all, keep your love for
one another at full strength, since love
covers a multitude of sins.

1 Peter 4:8

You might be relieved to know that we can love others without feeling all warm and fuzzy. One of the distinctions of *agape,* the Greek word most commonly translated "love" in the New Testament, is the active participation of the will.

In other words, *agape* is a love that's not only exercised when we feel like it. It is exercised when we choose to extend God's love as an act of our will—often a sacrificial act of our will. Sometimes our only motivation for doing so is obedience to God. But when we're willing, we're succinctly told in 1 Corinthians 13:8 that "love never fails."

If you do not stand
firm in your faith, then you
will not stand at all.
Isaiah 7:9

God seems to work in themes with me.
I wonder if you've experienced something similar. "Love Me" seemed to be
His theme for my twenties; "Love Me
and Know Me" for my thirties; "Love Me,
Know Me, and Believe Me" became His
mouthful for my forties.

"Believe Me." These two words now
echo unceasingly in my mind.

Faith is the way believers jump on
board with God and participate in countless wonderful things He has a mind to
do. And faith is what happens when believers *believe*—not just here and there in
crises but as a lifestyle. "Believe Me."

He has given us very great and
precious promises, so that through them
you may share in the divine nature.

2 Peter 1:4

Beloved, God has made us many wonderful promises. Real ones. Numerous ones. Promises of things like all-surpassing power, productivity, peace, and joy, even while occupying these jars of clay. Few of us will argue the theory, but why aren't more of us living the reality? Would we know His blessing if we saw it?

Blessing is defined by neither ease nor worldly possessions nor pain-free existence nor stock-market successes. Blessing is bowing down to receive the expressions of divine favor that in the inner recesses of the human heart make life worth the bother.

They all ate the same spiritual food, and all
drank the same spiritual drink. . . . But God
was not pleased with most of them.

1 Corinthians 10:3–5

Unbelief. That was the problem with the
children of Israel after the exodus from
Egypt. Oh, they believed in God. Their
oversight was that they didn't believe the
God they believed in. They talked a good
talk, but their walk did nothing but tread
sandal tracks in the desert.

God promised His chosen people
land, blessing, productivity, victory. But
the masses never saw their theology become reality. The question raised in the
wilderness was not whether Israel belonged to God or where they would spend
eternity. The question was where they
would spend their earthly existence.

Don't go near it, so that you can
see the way to go, for you haven't
traveled this way before.

Joshua 3:4

When the children of Israel were gathered on the banks of the Jordan with the
Promised Land in sight, God gave Joshua
instructions for their departure from the
wilderness. They were to follow the ones
carrying the ark of the covenant, "for you
haven't traveled this way before."

Even those who practice a highly active belief in God haven't already arrived
at every God-scheduled destination. If
they had, He would have already swept
them up to heaven, where our faith walk
ends. Like the Israelites, we've still got
places to go with God. And we've never
been this way before.

Among all the wise people of the
nations and among all their kingdoms,
there is no one like You.
Jeremiah 10:7

I don't think the biggest threat to our
theology is humanism or the host of
world religions. Our biggest threat is
cut-and-paste Christianity. If man places
his faith in a god he has recreated in his
own image, has he placed his faith in God
at all?

On the other hand, a man or woman
can believe enough of Scripture to accept
Christ as Savior but refuse to accept who
He additionally says He is. I am Keith's
wife, but what if he didn't accept the fact
that I was also the mother of his children?
With a broken heart, I would wonder
how he could say he knows me at all.

Keep asking, and it will be given to you.
Keep searching, and you will find. Keep
knocking, and the door will be opened.
Matthew 7:7

One reason why we witness fewer miracles and wonders today is because we are a dreadfully unbelieving generation, particularly in the prosperous West. Reports of miracles come out of Third World countries where all they have is faith.

The reason I can spot unbelieving believers pretty readily is because it takes one to know one. I was at the front of the line for many years. But we are caught in a tragic cycle. We believe little because we see little, so we see little and continue to believe little. It's time we dropped this wobbling cycle for a form of transportation that really gets us somewhere.

Let us lay aside every weight and the sin that so easily ensnares us . . . keeping our eyes on Jesus, the source and perfecter of our faith.

Hebrews 12:1–2

Though I know that wonders haven't ceased because I've seen and experienced them myself, I won't argue that according to His sovereignty, God may have greater purpose and higher priorities for widespread miracles in some generations and geographies than others.

But my argument is that we could use some profound works of God in our here and now, and He may just be waiting for us to muster up some corporate belief and start asking Him. Why can't the day of miracles be now? Why must it wait? Could God even now be waiting for a fresh revival of faith?

Jesus said to her, "Didn't I tell you
that if you believed you would
see the glory of God?"
John 11:40

Don't lose heart and think you already
see the handwriting on the wall: "I may
as well accept that God will be most glorified by my not getting the miracle I so
desperately want or think I need." Check
out Scripture! God was often glorified
through the miracle that blessed only
temporally.

To Martha, who was grieving the
death of her brother, Christ revealed His
glory by raising Lazarus from the dead.
Don't assume to know how God will be
most glorified. Ask for the miracle, and
let our sovereign, wise, and long-range
planning God measure the glory.

You did not receive a spirit of
slavery to fall back into fear, but you
received the Spirit of adoption.
Romans 8:15

If our stubborn minds would absorb that
we are accepted by God because of Jesus
Christ, our choices and subsequent behaviors would be profoundly affected.

Think about the impact of this for a
moment. What is a bigger contributor to
consistent defeat than insecurity? How
many foolish decisions does it motivate?
I made some of my worst choices in an
attempt to be accepted.

In our search for the root of our self-
destructive tendencies, all we have to do
is follow the stem of insecurities. But no
matter how long we've been in bondage
to it, we don't have to stay that way.

Put on the full armor of God
so that you can stand against
the tactics of the Devil.
Ephesians 6:11

I remember when one of my dear friend's sons tried out for the football team. He was so thin the pads just made him look normal. And his first game was against a team who obviously ate their Wheaties.

The first time a large player ran toward him, he steeled himself for the hit. But in the split second before collision, a survival reflex seemed to take over. He stepped aside and motioned as if to say, "By all means, go right ahead."

Don't think for a moment that Satan is going to slow down when he sees you in the way. Prepare yourself in advance so you won't be caught off guard.

My word that comes from My mouth
will not return to Me empty, but it will
accomplish what I please.

Isaiah 55:11

God doesn't speak just to hear the sound
of His own voice. Neither does He speak
to be heard by others. He speaks in order
to accomplish.

It's a fact. God's Word possesses accomplishing power and achieving power.
But I want it to have accomplishing and
achieving power in me, in us. Thankfully,
so does God. One of the most prominent
changes we can make in our approach to
God is becoming very intentional about
thanking Him for the quickening power
of His Word, claiming and believing that
He is energizing it to achieve His desires,
even at the moment we receive it.

If anyone does not stumble in
what he says, he is a mature man who is
also able to control his whole body.

James 3:2

I'd like to suggest to you that we have
no greater built-in vessel for the external expression of divine power than our
mouths. Perhaps that's why Satan will
do anything he can to set the tongue
aflame with the fire of hell (James 3:6).
He knows that whoever holds the tongue
can often hold the whole man.

The tongues of God's people are
meant to be set ablaze by the holy fire
of heaven, achieving that which glori-
fies God. But a sanctified mouth is too
unnatural to ever be coincidental. If we
want it, we need to pursue it regularly
and cooperate with God to receive it.

In accordance with what is written,
"I believed, therefore I spoke," we also
believe, and therefore speak.

2 Corinthians 4:13

Communication is the essence of relationship, and words are its clearest means. Imagine what could happen if we allowed God to take authority of our mouths and infuse our words with His power. Think about the positive impact we could have on our circumstances, our mates, our children, our neighbors, co-workers, friends, and those we serve.

Scripture tells us that if Christ's words are dwelling in us, the Holy Spirit will often effect powerful results when we pray and speak what we believe. Yes, power is applied when we speak in His name with faith.

Come, you who are blessed by My Father,
inherit the kingdom prepared for you from
the foundation of the world.

Matthew 25:34

If you got deeply involved with Christ
when you came to know Him—not just
dabbling around or practicing your faith
in halfhearted fashion—then you have a
memorable history with Him no matter
how brief your relationship with Christ
has been.

The more you look back, however,
the more you will see that He was also at
work in you long before you accepted His
Son as your Savior. He has undoubtedly
been faithful to you, and your active remembrance of His faithfulness yesterday
will greatly increase your willingness to
trust Him today.

The LORD your God is testing you to know
whether you love the LORD your God with
all your heart and all your soul.

Deuteronomy 13:3

Everyone who has been delivered from
some area of bondage has also experienced times of testing. Whether or not
we will forget God's faithfulness is definitely among the tests we're sure to face.

But whatever the course exam, the
pop quizzes preparing us for it may include both successes and failures. Few
Christians operate entirely at the extreme of no belief or unwavering belief. I
believe God continues to test us in every
area until we pass. Sometimes He even
insists on an A. But He doesn't sit upon
His throne with a fly swatter waiting to
smack us at the first hint of doubt.

Affliction produces endurance,
endurance produces proven character, and
proven character produces hope.

Romans 5:3–4

Sometimes we lay a crucial request before God, perhaps a life-and-death matter, and we want something fast and spectacular. Instead, God often directs us to keep walking around that Jericho day after day, repeating the same fundamental steps while nothing seems to happen.

Oh, it will. We must never stop believing it will. But in the meantime, we've got to keep walking and keep circling no matter how many times we've done it before and no matter how many times we're yet to do it. We may want a constant dose of dramatics, but God enjoys seeing the perseverance of simple, daily devotion.

The great dragon was thrown out—
the ancient serpent . . . the Devil and Satan,
the one who deceives the whole world.
Revelation 12:9

We've got a battle to fight if we're going to experience the victory God has prepared for us, and He wants us to dent the very gates of hell along the way.

There's no doubt, though, that fighting the good fight of faith takes energy! But then so do self-pity, anger, unforgiveness, and self-loathing. Each of us must decide where we're going to put our energy when the battle grows fierce.

Satan knows that "the One who is in you is greater than the one who is in the world" (1 John 4:4). He just hopes you don't know it, that he can distract you from painting the bull's-eye on him.

It always protects, always trusts,
always hopes, always perseveres.
Love never fails.

1 Corinthians 13:7–8 (NIV)

I used to think this verse meant that love wouldn't fail to bring about the exact results I wanted. But "fail" actually portrays something that drops to the ground, thereby having no effect.

So with a better grasp on the concept these days, I can make you a bold, biblical promise: When you really love—difficultly and sacrificially—it never falls to the ground. Never. Not once. Not ever. God catches it even if no one else does. According His Word, we are incapable of loving in Jesus' name and for the sake of His sacrificial legacy for nothing. Love absolutely cannot fail.

Indeed, we have all
received grace after grace
from His fullness.
John 1:16

Learning to practice action-verb faith in the midst of terribly difficult circumstances has been the most exhilarating adventure I've ever had. In words truer to my sanguine nature, it's been a blast. Not the trials, mind you, but the invitation to believe God for victory—and even favor—in the middle of them.

Oh yes, I've seen miracles. Some of them have been huge. But God's daily interventions have been what awed me the most and left me shaking my head that the God of the universe would be so attentive to my trivial challenges. Try Him and see if your experience is the same.

Dear friends, do not believe
every spirit, but test the spirits to
determine if they are from God.

1 John 4:1

Wise you are if you want to "test" the
spirit and proceed with caution on subject matter such as "Believing God." I am
as reluctant to pick up books on faith as
anyone could possibly be. We live in a religious culture where faith practices have
been distorted and twisted to serve man
rather than God.

Our dilemma is whether or not
we will allow the misuse of the topic to
keep us from appropriate practices of
faith. Bear in mind that most heresies
are merely truths that have been twisted.
Trust the Word to unravel it for you and
to see it put into powerful practice.

Therefore, while the promise remains
of entering His rest, let us fear so that
none of you should miss it.
Hebrews 4:1

Like the children of Israel, I believe
many of us are wandering in the wilderness with the Promised Land just on the
other side of the river. I'd like to suggest that God not only approves of New
Testament believers applying the concept of a Promised Land, He insists on
it. Our Promised Land and Sabbath rest
may culminate in heaven, but an earthly
Promised Land exists for you and me.

Your Promised Land is the place
where God's personalized promises over
your life become a living reality rather
than a theological theory. He is inviting
you to move there and to flourish.

Now you, man of God, run from these
things; but pursue righteousness, godliness,
faith, love, endurance, and gentleness.

1 Timothy 6:11

God places a huge premium on living,
breathing faith. In fact, the more you
search the Scriptures, the more you discover that nothing is more important to
God than our faith.

But God is not the only one who puts
a high priority on this issue of our faith.
Satan also has no greater focus in a single
one of our lives. Though he is no match
for God, he is a powerful and dangerous
foe of believing man and woman.

Not coincidentally, then—because
the stakes are so high—both God and the
devil are targeting our faith. They know
faith works. We need to know it too.

Fight the good fight for the faith; take hold
of eternal life, to which you were called and
have made a good confession.

1 Timothy 6:12

The shield is the armor's armor. The ancient warrior hoped the fiery dart never reached the helmet or the breastplate. A direct hit on any of the other defensive covers could still stun and bruise even if it didn't wound. His goal was to extinguish any oncoming dart with his shield in order to diffuse potential damage.

The same is true in *our* warfare. The toughest battles in our lives will invariably concern matters of faith—times when we're tempted to think God's Word and His ways won't work for us, that He has abandoned us or failed to come through for us. Lift high your shield of faith.

You have done these things, and I kept silent;
you thought I was just like you. But I will
rebuke you and lay out the case before you.

Psalm 50:21

I believe one reason why we default to a
lesser-God theology is our arrogant determination to define God differently
than He defines Himself. All human attempts to define God cannot help but
minimize Him.

We somehow want to neatly package God and make everything about Him
explainable. We then decide that what's
not explainable is not plausible. We try
to make Him fit into our textbooks. We
want Him to calm down, not be so . . .
God-ish. We decide we will only believe
what we can humanly reconcile. And as a
result, we abandon the way of faith.

APRIL

Trust in the LORD with all
your heart, and do not rely on
your own understanding.
Proverbs 3:5

I have a friend who has struggled with extreme highs and lows, a malady finally diagnosed as bipolar disorder. From what she described, I'm not sure today's church couldn't be diagnosed with a spiritual case of something similar.

Two diametrically opposed teachings exist on the subject of faith and miracles, making us one body with a divided mind. The magnetic power pulling Christians to one extreme or the other is overwhelming. But so is man's insecure desire to be doctrinally black and white. We find great security in *always* and *never;* hence, our bipolar existence.

The LORD said to Gideon, "I will deliver
you with the 300 men who lapped. . . .
But everyone else is to go home."
Judges 7:7

We are certainly not the first generation
missing widespread wonders. Gideon's
generation found itself under terrible
enemy oppression. They hid in strongholds and fell into an ineffectiveness far
removed from their promised position.
Impoverished, the Israelites cried out to
the Lord for help. The rest is history.

But the precedent that God set in
Gideon's generation offers me no small
encouragement for today. Even if the
masses do not welcome God to pour
out a fresh anointing of faith upon His
church, He can still perform wonders
through a small army.

Our momentary light affliction
is producing for us an absolutely
incomparable eternal weight of glory.
2 Corinthians 4:17

My friend Jennifer Rothschild is a singer and musician who writes, teaches Bible studies on video, and is the essence of grace and beauty. She has it all . . . except for one thing. Jennifer is blind.

She would very much like to have her sight. She makes no bones about it. The complications of blindness are endless as she raises two boys she can't see. Yet in eternity, we'll have plenty of chances to ask Jennifer if she would have traded in her blindness for a life of mediocrity and greater independence from God. I think we can expect her to say no. She cooperated with God and got a greater yes.

He put a new song in my mouth,
a hymn of praise to our God. Many will see
and fear, and put their trust in the LORD.

Psalm 40:3

I have a pretty messy conglomeration of early childhood victimization and a long-term history of defeat to thank for my deep insecurity and uncertainty. Actually, "self-torment" would be a better word for it. I suppose it's the residual of a formerly self-destructive nature. Whatever it is, it waves like a red flag to the enemy: "Hit her right here! This is where she's weakest! Aim here!"

God has to be omnipotent to have kept me out of the ditch for as long as He has, but just as surely, He was also omnipotent through my tumbles. Every time we fall, He is able to help us up.

Do not be afraid or discouraged,
for the LORD your God is with
you wherever you go.
Joshua 1:9

God warned Joshua in the verse above not to fall for two of the most effective deterrents to a Promised Land existence: fear and discouragement.

Fear is the very factor that keeps many of us from fleshing out the biblical reality that we can "do all things through Christ" (Phil 4:13). We *can* do all things through Christ who strengthens us, but frankly we *won't* if we're too afraid to try.

Satan will do anything he can to scare us away from our God-ordained destinies. We must be on guard against the arsenal of psychological weapons he uses to keep our feet off promised ground.

He replied to them, "My mother
and My brothers are those who hear
and do the word of God."
Luke 8:21

As I sit before God on my back porch
every morning, placing that day's sched-
ule and petitions before Him in prayer,
I receive my daily Bible reading like an
athlete might eat an energy bar. I often
read that day's portion aloud and actively
participate in receiving it into my belief
system. I take a moment to meditate on
it, asking God to sow these words deep
into my otherwise deceptive heart and
even into my subconscious mind.

I count on those morning Scriptures
to become active, energizing, and powerful in me that day. And they do. Because
that's what they were meant to do.

The revealed things belong to us
and our children forever, so that we may
follow all the words of this law.

Deuteronomy 29:29

One of the primary ways God sanctifies
our tongues is to put His Word on it. As
we've already seen, the first strategy God
gave Joshua for living victoriously and
successfully in the Promised Land was
the command not to let the book of the
Law "depart from [his] mouth" (Josh.
1:8). God wanted His Word to be on the
tip of Joshua's tongue!

The Old Testament idea of meditation did not involve the thought life alone
but also the mouth, repeating a precept
of Scripture, talking it over while reflect-
ing and thinking on it. May His Word be
continually on our lips, as well.

Do not despise the LORD's instruction . . .
for the LORD disciplines the one He loves,
just as a father, the son he delights in.
Proverbs 3:11–12

When we're actively trying to do what God says we can, yet we're consistently not getting the results His Word says we can expect, we are wise to consider possible obstacles. If our words continue to bear little fruit, the hindrance could be an unsanctified tongue.

As you consider the potential power blockage, keep in mind that your goal is to identify and remove hindrances to practicing the powerful voice God's Word tells us we can have. Feeling guilty or defeated is not the goal. His purposes are always redemptive, even when He is leading us to confront hard truth.

A book of remembrance was written
before Him for those who feared Yahweh
and had high regard for His name.
Malachi 3:16

In order to strengthen our faith muscles,
we should exert a little energy reflect-
ing upon and memorializing times when
God has openly demonstrated His faithfulness to us.

Think of the Israelites' path through
the Jordan River as the step-by-step process through which God led His people
to the Promised Land. See where you can
retrace God's goodness to you.

Perhaps you've never forgotten many
of His faithful acts, but have you ever actually recorded them? Will your children
and descendants have any kind of written record of their heritage of faith?

Carefully consider the path
for your feet, and all your ways
will be established.
Proverbs 4:26

I lived much of my life in a continuous cycle of defeat. Sin would always bring heartbreak. I'd confess and repent with all the energy I had. Then sooner or later, I'd cycle back into another pit.

But belief finally prevailed and the old cycle broke. He retested me in some past areas of defeat, and *finally* I began passing more than failing, believing more than disbelieving. Prevailing belief led me to a far more consistent state of abiding.

The same will be true of you on your own timetable with God. If you have not yet experienced this, I pray you will not rest until God takes you there.

You are to labor six days and do
all your work, but the seventh day is a
Sabbath to the LORD your God.
Exodus 20:9–10

G. K. Chesterton wrote of a God who "is strong enough to exult in monotony. It is possible that God says every morning, 'Do it again' to the sun; and every evening, 'Do it again' to the moon. . . . It may be that God makes every daisy separately, but has never got tired of making them."

Ours is a God who delights in a perfect concoction of creativity and order. Though He could have thought the entire cosmos into existence in a millisecond, He brought it about with great patience in six distinct increments. Then rested on the seventh. Then later insisted that His children do the same.

See to it that no one falls short of the grace of God and that no root of bitterness springs up, causing trouble and by it, defiling many.

Hebrews 12:15

God alone can give us the daily dose of grace not to grow bitter in a long-term battle. But Satan will do everything he can to try keeping us from receiving the grace God extends.

One of his usual approaches is trying to convince us that God withholds His help after the fact if we didn't ask for it before. He wants us to believe that God is sitting on His throne huffing, "You got yourself into this mess; you can get yourself out." Beloved, I assure you that some of the most awesome things God has ever done for me have come out of the most awful things I'd done to myself.

I have labored in vain, I have spent my
strength for nothing and futility; yet my
vindication is with the LORD.

Isaiah 49:4

Every effort we make to love sacrificially
never fails to get the priority attention of
God, to ultimately and undoubtedly be
rewarded, and to have a profound effect
either in the person we are trying to love
or in the circumstance. Or in us.

And maybe even in God. Have you
ever considered that when He took the
chance of loving us, He also took the
risk of being affected by us? Tears still
sting my eyes when I think about situations where loving didn't yield the results
I wanted. But my soul's consolation is
knowing that none of the work fell to the
ground. It's in God's hands. So is yours.

If you remain in Me and My words
remain in you, ask whatever you want
and it will be done for you.
John 15:7

I finally came to a point in my Christian
walk where I grew bone weary of inconsistency being my only constant in life.
Occasional wisps of authentic spiritual
living only multiplied my frustrations. I
knew a place of fullness and effectiveness
in Christ existed, but at best I was only a
drop-in.

My soul needed a place it could live.
I longed for my defeats to be infrequent
visitations, not my victories. Beloved, our
personalized lands of earthly promise are
places we're invited by God to dwell in
Christ. It's high time we stopped dropping in and started taking up residency.

You have created all things,
and because of Your will they
exist and were created.
Revelation 4:11

We may as well accept faith challenges as a fact of life and not be shocked or feel picked on when they come. God brings them to build our faith, prove us genuine, and afford Himself endless excuses to reward us. He delights in nothing more than our choice to believe Him over what we see and feel.

The verse above adds an important dimension to our understanding of why God derives pleasure in our exercise of faith. Our ultimate purpose for existence is to please Him; therefore, if we don't exercise faith, we will never fulfill our reason for being.

Joshua told the people, "Consecrate
yourselves, because the LORD will do
wonders among you tomorrow."
Joshua 3:5

I love the definition of the Hebrew word
pala, translated "wonders" in this verse
from Joshua 3. In effect, God was saying
to the Israelites, "If you set yourself apart
to Me, I will distinguish Myself to you
in ways more wonderful and miraculous
than you have ever imagined."

I want to behold and experience any
wonder God is willing to reveal to me. I
not only want to have faith enough for
God to grant me my Promised Land,
I want to see amazing exploits of God
while I'm there. If so, then, my life needs
to be consecrated through an active pursuit of increasing personal holiness.

God, be exalted above
the heavens; let Your glory
be above the whole earth.
Psalm 57:5

Our pride and desperation to feel smart can make us unwilling to answer theological questions with the only human answer that exists to some of them: "I don't know. But I know that what He says is true even when I can't explain it or reconcile it with what has happened."

All attempts at taking away the mystery and wonder that surround God leave Him something He is not. We cannot tame the Lion of Judah. There is a mystery, a wonder, and, yes, even a wildness about God we cannot take away from Him. Nor would we want to if we could somehow grasp the adventure of Him.

We speak God's hidden wisdom
in a mystery, which God predestined
before the ages for our glory.
1 Corinthians 2:7

The Bible describes a God who is a thousand things to His children, even though some of these are beyond our ability to understand. So when people insist on humanly reasonable theologies to satisfy their need to believe, the lesser god they're buying is not the God of Scripture. We must beware of recreating an image of God that makes us feel better.

Of this I'm certain: If in our pursuit of greater knowledge God seems to have gotten smaller, we have been deceived, no matter how intelligent the deceiver seems or how well-meaning and sincere his or her doctrine.

We don't see any signs for us.
There is no longer a prophet. . . .
Why do You hold back Your hand?
Psalm 74:9, 11

God's people have long searched for missing miracles. The psalmists, who had heard with their ears but desperately wanted to see with their eyes, intimated that when God withheld wonders, His thinking people assumed something was wrong, and the wise rightly searched for the disconnection.

If in reality we are seeing fewer wonders of God in the midst of His people and through His people, shouldn't we as well inquire why? Are we not equally desperate? Is God no longer willing to intervene miraculously and wondrously in our behalf?

We have this treasure in clay jars,
so that this extraordinary power may
be from God and not from us.

2 Corinthians 4:7

The ministry of the new covenant is the ministry of the Holy Spirit not just around, upon, and with believers but also inside believers. Jesus spoke of the Holy Spirit to His disciples when He said, "He remains with you and will be in you" (John 14:17).

Meditate on the difference between "with" and "in." The difference turned a band of fumbling scaredy-cats in the Gospel records into unparalleled power-houses in the book of Acts and beyond. And the same work of the Spirit applies to us. The new covenant is an inward work with glorious manifestations.

Those He predestined, He also called;
and those He called, He also justified; and
those He justified, He also glorified.

Romans 8:30

All of us who are believers in Christ have a calling. I am convinced God assigns our callings for a host of reasons, many of which serve a purpose in *us,* not just in those we will serve. God is the master of multitasking.

I don't think He'd be offended if I said that He purposely picks on something until He can get it to the surface. For example, God knew that what He called me to do would force me to deal with the deeply embedded thorns of my past. Therefore, our callings can be at stake if we are not willing to allow Him to deal with our insecurities.

Moses responded to the people, "Don't be afraid, for God has come to test you, so that you will fear Him and will not sin."

Exodus 20:20

I have wrestled with a stronghold of fear much of my life. Like you, the combination of life's challenges and a long list of loved ones provide the enemy no few opportunities to prey on my fears.

I have often heard the statistic that 90 percent of what we fear never comes to pass. Those statistics have certainly proved true in my experience, but God has taught me as much from the 10 percent as the 90. In fact, one of the ways God has cured my fears is by allowing a few of them to come to fruition. After the crisis came and went, He seemed to ask, "Beth, did you live through it?"

Let the hearts of those who seek the
LORD rejoice. Search for the LORD and for
His strength; seek His face always.
1 Chronicles 16:10–11

I have loved God's Word for a long time,
but my approach and expectation have
changed dramatically as my confidence in
Him has grown. In the old days, I used to
expect a little direction and the increase
of a little knowledge from my daily Bible
reading. Therefore, those were the dividends I was most aware of receiving.

But I now add to those expectations
things like liveliness, energy, and empow-
erment from the Word, counting on its
effectiveness in advance. As I go through
my day, meeting inevitable challenges
and self-doubts, I depend on and expect
Him to be strong in me. And He is.

"Is not My word like fire"—
the LORD's declaration—"and like
a sledgehammer that pulverizes rock?"
Jeremiah 23:29

Having God's Word ready on the tip of
our tongues has numerous advantages,
one of which my husband, Keith, vividly
illustrated the day he shot the head off a
rattlesnake who had slithered across our
path while we walked in the country.

As long as we're armed, we can walk
along leisurely and peacefully, because at
a moment's notice we are ready to shoot
the head off that "ancient serpent, who is
called the Devil and Satan" (Rev. 12:9).
Yes, having God's Word on our hearts
and on our lips is like having a loaded gun
with us on our walks to and through our
Promised Lands.

Jesus told him, "Go away, Satan!
For it is written: 'Worship the Lord your
God, and serve only Him.'"
Matthew 4:10

Looking back to the rattlesnake story I
mentioned yesterday, think of the head
of the snake as representing authority. A
stronghold is any way the devil tries to
presume authority in our lives. If we belong to Christ, he has no right to exercise
authority over us, but he hopes we're too
ignorant regarding Scripture to know it.
He hopes our gun isn't loaded.

In the wilderness of temptation,
Christ set the best example of respond-
ing with the Word of God when under
satanic assault. Knowing and claiming
God's Word when attacked blows the
head off enemy forces.

Out of the same mouth come
blessing and cursing. My brothers, these
things should not be this way.
James 3:10

When Christ empowered His disciples
to speak under His authority and to effect certain results, He treated the tongue
as an instrument. The muscle itself has
no spiritual power, of course. The understanding is that the Holy Spirit infuses
power through it.

God can use our tongues to bring
about stunning results, whether immediately or over time. He is not, however,
likely to regularly infuse an instrument
that is also employed for opposing purposes. In other words, the wrong use of
the instrument can dramatically hinder
its effectiveness with the right use.

I will remember the LORD's works;
yes, I will remember Your ancient wonders.
I will reflect on all You have done.

Psalm 77:11–12

I'd like to ask you to join me in personal-
izing the psalmist's words and apply his
historical reference to "ancient wonders"
to your own personal "long ago."

Try glancing back to see what trea-
sures you can find, sometimes even in
the midst of rubble. Like detectives at a
scene, start looking for any visible finger-
prints of your invisible God interspersed
throughout your life.

He has been there all along, Beloved,
even before you acknowledged Him as
Savior. He is the living, infinite, eternal,
omnipresent God who woos to His heart
those who will draw near.

If we live by the Spirit, we must also follow the Spirit. We must not become conceited, provoking one another, envying one another.

Galatians 5:25–26

No cycle—either of victory or defeat—is necessarily permanent as long as we dwell on this earth. Our patterns or cycles can change and spiral up . . . or revert and spiral down. Unfortunately, the Israelites did not abide in the freedom and prosperity of their Promised Land indefinitely. The idolatry and disobedience that later led to Assyrian and Babylonian captivity grew from roots of prevailing unbelief.

You and I don't have to follow suit. The Spirit of the living Christ abides in us, bearing faithfulness as fruit. We won't walk in *perfect* faith for the rest of our lives, but we can walk in prevailing faith.

At daybreak, LORD, You hear
my voice; at daybreak I plead my case
to You and watch expectantly.

Psalm 5:3

I have lived too much of my life in defeat to risk living in a gray zone. Certain disciplines are a part of my life, and to do otherwise—no matter how I'd label it—is disobedience. But though my morning almost always begins at the same table and chair, the sunrise surrounding me could be any number of colors. There is creativity even in sameness.

So sometimes I jump up and down; sometimes I go prostrate to the ground. Sometimes I pray Scripture. Other times I pray moans and groans. But pray, I must. It's God's will even when I can't tell if it's changing a thing.

This is the confidence we have
before Him: whenever we ask anything
according to His will, He hears us.

1 John 5:14

Whether the circumstances that led to our fiercest battles are someone else's fault, our own fault, or the fruit of life's unfairness, having God as our Father grants us this hope: a perfect setup for catastrophic defeat is also the perfect setup for miraculous victory. No matter how we got into this mess, we just have to keep believing.

Those who decide to be preoccupied with believing God over all their negative emotions and other feelings to the contrary will sooner or later discover that God delights in answered prayer, no matter how big those prayers become.

MAY

Hope does not disappoint, because God's
love has been poured out in our hearts
through the Holy Spirit who was given to us.
Romans 5:5

Love is not a spiritual gift. Otherwise we'd all conveniently claim not to possess that particular anointing. Rather, love is a supreme and priority calling: the fruit of the Spirit of Christ within us that surfaces when we are filled by Him, yielded to His authority.

The chief reason we find loving so painful, aggravating, and fruitless is because we keep trying to love with the pitifully small resources of our own emotional tank. The only way to love others—our spouses, our enemies, our in-laws, our betrayers, our parents—is by faith, not by feeling. We love by faith!

The LORD your God is bringing you into a
good land . . . where you will eat food without shortage, where you will lack nothing.
Deuteronomy 8:7, 9

As much as any other characteristic of
the Promised Land, God said it would be
fruitful. Many of us have heard it charac-
terized as a land of "milk and honey," but
additional Scriptures (like Deuteronomy
8:7–9) are far more descriptive.

This is not a description of *some* fruit
but of *much* fruit, as is the description
from John 15:8 about our bearing fruit as
Jesus' disciples. Yes, your Father wants to
show His glory by bearing tremendous
fruit through you. Your personalized
Promised Land is the abiding place where
you get to see God keep the promise of a
great harvest through your life.

Keep the LORD's commands
and statutes I am giving you today,
for your own good.
Deuteronomy 10:13

Especially if you haven't yet developed a trust relationship with God, the concept of living your entire life to please Him may unnerve or even offend you. Believe me, I understand.

I, too, have battled tremendous trust issues in every relational dimension. I have not always found man (nor myself) to be trustworthy, but I can say that God has never failed to live up to His Word in our relationship. I believe you will find Him trustworthy, too.

God is for us, Dear One. Even His commands (as Deuteronomy 10:13 says) are for our safety, liberty, and blessing.

When Jesus came to the region of Caesarea
Philippi, He asked His disciples, "Who do
people say that the Son of Man is?"
Matthew 16:13

I can't count the mothers who have told
me they were looking for a Christian
school where their children could get "a
good eduction and learn a little something about God." Be careful that your
children are not learning that God is a
"little something."

There is no such thing as a flawless
church or a flawless Christian school or
university, because they are full of flawed
people just like me. But we don't have to
accept a lesser-God theology just because
it's prevalent. We can make our own life's
pursuit the God of Scripture, not just
who man says He is.

Will You prolong Your anger for all
generations? Will You not revive us again
so that Your people may rejoice in You?
Psalm 85:5–6

We are surrounded by a dying, depraved
world, mounting violence, the threat of
mass destruction, and a surging fury of
satanic assault and seduction. We are told
churches are in terrible decline. Many
pastors and leaders are depressed.

We are desperate for the wonders
and miracles of God. We need Him to
show His mighty arm and tell the world
that He is alive, active, and very much
with us. We need more than the best pro-
grams and planning can accomplish. Oh,
that we would fall on our faces and cry
out to God for more than we may even
have the courage or imagination to ask.

Let us be glad, rejoice, and give Him glory,
because the marriage of the Lamb has come,
and His wife has prepared herself.
Revelation 19:7

I believe God's greatest priorities in the age between the establishment of the New Testament church and the latter days are internal ones. Therefore, one of the chief responsibilities of the bride of Christ in this age is to make herself ready for Jesus, her Bridegroom.

Christ will return for a pure bride, a state of being that necessitates deep, internal works. God's eyes are fastened with eternal intentions on the inner man. That's why sometimes God may prioritize performing a miracle on our hearts and minds over a miracle concerning our circumstances.

The LORD will strike Egypt, striking and
healing. Then they will return to the LORD
and He will hear their prayers.

Isaiah 19:22

If God wanted to force me to face my insecurities head-on, He certainly chose an
effective calling for me. Trust me on this:
if you're insecure, you don't want to stand
up in front of an audience and speak. Nor
do you want to turn in a manuscript to
editors. What I've been called to do ex-
poses me constantly to criticism—both
constructive and otherwise.

But His reason for surfacing the
destructive parts of us is so we will face
them and cooperate as He uproots and
heals our wounds. God will put you in a
position to wrestle with your identity and
choose whom you believe: Him or you.

Therefore, I will most gladly boast
all the more about my weaknesses, so that
Christ's power may reside in me.
2 Corinthians 12:9

Every now and then I ask those gathered in an audience how many have gotten through something that they believed beforehand they couldn't bear. Hands never fail to raise all over the auditorium.

Living through something we were sure we couldn't endure gives us a small glimpse of our inner man's immortality and is clear evidence that the "I can do all things through Christ who strengthens me" promise works for us, too. None of us particularly like the face-it-until-you-get-over-it approach to fear banishment, but it can certainly be effective. Yes, you can make it, God and you.

Pay attention to my words; listen closely to my sayings. . . . For they are life to those who find them, and health to one's whole body.

Proverbs 4:20, 22

When I study God's Word, I often ask that He'll make me a healthier person in any way He sees fit as a direct result. I ask the same thing for my children and my husband. Likewise, I ask God to send forth His healing words to those who participate in the Bible studies He has given me.

I will joyfully receive any application of that precept He desires, whether it is a work toward spiritual, emotional, mental, or physical wholeness. I continually count on God's Word accomplishing greater wholeness in every true hearer, no matter what form it takes.

All Scripture is inspired by God and
is profitable for teaching, for rebuking, for
correcting, for training in righteousness.
2 Timothy 3:16

We can read the Scripture for hours, but
if we don't receive it by faith, it doesn't
abide in us, bringing its vitality, energy,
and effectiveness. We may be encouraged by it, but we are neither empowered
nor changed.

But if we do receive it by faith—
thereby accepting it into our belief system—we might think of the practice like
inhaling a breath of faith, like receiving
spiritual CPR. Then when we choose to
speak what we believe, we might think
of ourselves as exhaling that same breath
into speech, speaking it over our specific
circumstances.

I will meditate on Your precepts and
think about Your ways. I will delight in Your
statutes; I will not forget Your word.
Psalm 119:15–16

It's true that making a reasonable, livable
lifestyle of believing and speaking God's
Word is like living on the CPR of the
Holy Spirit. Don't try to make something
mystical out of this. Actually, nothing is
more practical. The idea is that the more
we believe the Word and then take the
opportunity to speak that same Word,
concept, or application, the more we actively live and breath faith.

This practice can take place through
reading Scripture aloud, memorizing it,
meditating on it, or seizing opportunities to discuss it with others. Try some of
these yourself today.

Rid yourselves of all
wickedness, all deceit, hypocrisy,
envy, and all slander.

1 Peter 2:1

You and I want to be people to whom
God can entrust a spiritually powerful
voice. Let's allow the Holy Spirit to alert
us to some misuses of the tongue that can
greatly diffuse its spiritual effectiveness:

Gossip. Lying. Profanity. Perversity.
Unkindness. Complaining. Disrespect.
Negativism. Criticism. Breaking a confidence. Using inappropriate humor. De-
meaning others. Misuse of God's name—
not just taking His name in vain but using
it loosely, casually. We can only imagine
how reluctant God might be to infuse
our prayers with power when we use our
tongues for inappropriate purposes.

But the Counselor, the Holy Spirit . . .
will teach you all things and remind you
of everything I have told you.
John 14:26

Imagine all the spiritual implications of
an active memory in our walk with God.
Without a doubt, memory is a vital part
of the learning process and is also a vital
part of the faith-building process.

Perhaps you're already trying to
think back over your past, recalling specific evidences of God's activity. Though
you may be convinced He's been there
for you all along, you may be drawing a
mental blank on many precise instances.

But you can enlist the Holy Spirit's
help in remembering acts of God's faithfulness—the kind of positive memory re-
trieval that edifies rather than terrifies.

The LORD then said to Joshua,
"Today I have rolled away the
disgrace of Egypt from you."
Joshua 5:9

God wants to roll away all your disgrace
and reproach. But don't miss the fact that
God rolled away Israel's reproach after
reconfirming the rite of covenantal circumcision (Josh. 5:2) and observing their
obedience to His command.

Yes, a wounding of sorts took place
before the Israelites were released to live
fruitfully in their land of promise. Uh-
huh, been there. So have many others.
I don't know a single person who truly
seems to bear the mark of God's presence and power in his or her life who
hasn't been asked by God to be obedient
in a way that was dramatically painful.

You took off your former way of life, the old
man that is corrupted by deceitful desires . . .
being renewed in the spirit of your minds.

Ephesians 4:22–23

Think of our reproach as the vestiges of
what we still insisted on wearing from
our old wardrobe, whether these telltale
actions occurred before or after our salvation. At the risk of being a bit graphic,
it was that which Christ circumcised but
we tried to keep as a cover.

This wardrobe problem of ours (our
unwillingness to take off some things) is
a mental issue, really. Though we were totally changed on the inside when we were
made new creatures in Christ, our minds
often take time to be renewed. We're far
more likely to *act* like the old man of sin
when we still *feel* like him.

Satisfy us in the morning with
Your faithful love so that we may shout
with joy and be glad all our days.
Psalm 90:14

A long time ago I had to quit giving myself the option of whether or not to rise
in the morning for prayer and spend time
in the Word that day. These fundamentals are a part of my life. Though I may
practice these disciplines in different
ways, I do them virtually every day.

Why so? Because God seems to like
them. Picture God nudging you and
me awake before dawn because He can
hardly wait to be with us. Then as we
make our sleepy way to the usual meeting place, imagine Him saying something
rather like G. K. Chesterton suggested:
"Do it again, child!"

The sun stood still and the
moon stopped, until the nation took
vengeance on its enemies.

Joshua 10:13

Somewhere in the process of facing
five-to-one odds against the Canaanite
armies, Joshua received a word from God
that He was going to give them victory.
But don't think for a moment the Israelites could stand back and watch.

This wasn't a "be still" moment. Nor
was it a "stand still" moment. Certainly
it was a "wield your sword" moment,
but the relentless demand threw it into
a "100 percent/all you've got" moment.
God gave them an awesome victory, but
He required every ounce of energy and
cooperation they had in the process. He
does that sometimes.

Now these three remain:
faith, hope, and love. But the
greatest of these is love.
1 Corinthians 13:13

Living *agape* is a daily commitment of the will to vacate the premises of the heart with its own preferential affections, and to make its chambers a fleshy canteen for the liquid love of God.

Yes, it's still a challenge, but it's no longer the impossible dream. We live by faith. We love by faith. Faith and love are inseparable housemates that offer hospitality to hope. When we lose our faith to love, we lose the energy to love. Then we lose our hope.

Beloved, when all is said and done, living is for loving. This is our daily hope: faith expressing itself through love.

A land of wheat, barley, vines,
figs, and pomegranates; a land
of olive oil and honey.

Deuteronomy 8:8

God has far more in mind than bringing forth one kind of fruit from your life.
The harvest God desires to produce has
the potential of abounding variety.

You and I weren't called to become
machines of mass-but-monotonous pro-
duction. Just when we decide our lives
are all about figs, God starts mixing in
some pomegranates.

Have you too quickly decided that
what you've done or what you're doing is
all you'll ever do? Ah, God's far too creative for that. May He use your present
journey of life to shake up some soil and
show you what all can grow there.

The fruit of the light results in all
goodness, righteousness, and truth—
discerning what is pleasing to the Lord.
Ephesians 5:9–10

God calls us to surrender our own agendas on the altar of His will, knowing that His will for us is good, pleasing, and perfectly suited. When all is said and done, the biggest sacrifices of our lives will be the times when we chose our own way and forfeited God's pleasing will for us.

The last thing Satan wants, however, is for God to be pleased. Satan's ultimate gripe is with God. His chief goal is to get back at God for not putting up with his arrogance and his desire to be "like the Most High" (Isa. 14:14). He cannot touch God, so he does everything he can to get to His heart by getting to His children.

He touched their eyes,
saying, "Let it be done for you
according to your faith!"
Matthew 9:29

The pleasure of God is not the only premium at stake in our exercise of faith. Both God and Satan know that faith works. Its God-ordained dividends are astronomical. Unfortunately, so are the costs of its absence.

Biblically speaking, faith is without equal in its effects upon the human life, precisely because God is without equal and because faith is the normative invitation that He answers with proof. Christ can operate any way He desires in our lives, but His usual mode of operation regarding His followers is "according to your faith."

Even if we have known Christ
in a purely human way, yet now we
no longer know Him like that.
2 Corinthians 5:16

Great wisdom is found in having the courage to take an inventory of how we have developed our present perceptions of God and how biblically accurate they are. Many people and factors can influence who we've come to believe God is: our parents, our teachers, our friends, our enemies, our experiences, our health, our hardships. Many more come into play.

Have these factors led us to believe that God is who He says He is? Someone less? Or someone simply different? As we ask ourselves hard questions, keep in mind that faith unchallenged ordinarily remains unchanged.

LORD, Your name endures
forever, Your reputation, LORD,
through all generations.
Psalm 135:13

God has the power and authority to
grant anything on our list, A–Z. All the
resources of heaven belong to Him. Even
if something I've asked for necessitates a
miracle, without hesitation I believe my
God can accomplish it.

When I'm in heaven, however, I am
certain I will esteem the greatest miracle
of all to be godly offspring who brought
Him glory from such formerly sinful and
enslaved parents. God has performed
miracles in my behalf—even physical
healing—but Keith and I consider the
greatest miracle to be the way He is trans-
forming our family line. How about you?

For we also are weak in Him,
yet toward you we will live with
Him by God's power.
2 Corinthians 13:4

Perhaps like some of you, I remake the decision almost every single day to believe I am who God says I am. The fact that I have not refused this public vocation or quit when the going got tough is a testimony to the pure tenacity of God to demand that I believe Him.

I share this with you because I have a feeling some of you can relate. Has God placed you in a position that seems to stir up every insecurity you have? Take it personally, Dear One. He's stirring it up to scoop it out—often one spoonful at a time. This is the path He often takes on the way to our God-ordained destiny.

Since it was out of ignorance that I
had acted in unbelief, I received mercy,
and the grace of our Lord overflowed.

1 Timothy 1:13–14

I often associate certain songs with certain seasons of my life. One morning I
insisted to God that I could not bear a
set of circumstances that appeared inevitable in front of me. A song came to my
mind with the following lyric: "You're not
as strong as you think you are." Only this
time, one word was different: "You're not
as *weak* as you think you are."

Our insistence that "I could never
survive if that happened to me" is not only
an insult to the people who have already
survived something similar. It's an insult
to a wonderful thing called grace. Where
need abounds, grace more abounds.

Your words were found, and I ate them.
Your words became a delight to me
and the joy of my heart.
Jeremiah 15:16

If your expectation of God's Word in your life has been small, I ask you to consider giving it far more credit. Second Timothy 3:16 (NIV) says, "All Scripture is God-breathed," so don't just read it like any other inspirational or instructional text. Inhale it!

Try Jeremiah's approach while you're at it. Don't just *read* God's words. Receive them like a famished man at a feast. Ask God to cause it to abide in you and to bring its properties of effervescent life, power, and effectiveness with it. How about something moving into your life with some *positive* baggage for a change?

One generation will declare Your works to
the next and will proclaim Your mighty acts.
I will speak of . . . Your wonderful works.

Psalm 145:4–5

How does inhaling (through believing) and exhaling a fresh breath of faith (through speaking) work? I'm not suggesting berating people with Scripture. In terms of our analogy, we might call that "bad breath." A fresh word comes out of our mouths with fresh breath.

Remember: the Spirit of truth plus the Word of truth equals internal combustion. We take the passion and life of what is happening within us and externalize it through speech—not just for the sake of being heard but for the ultimate purpose of accomplishing and achieving in the image of our Creator.

Christ has liberated us into freedom.
Therefore stand firm and don't submit
again to a yoke of slavery.
Galatians 5:1

In various ways, all of us have blessed with one breath and cursed with the next. We've all been tempted to talk one way in our spiritual relationships and another way in our worldly relationships. Inconsistency may be common, but it is also costly. We pay the price with powerlessness more often than we know.

But living with less regret over our hastily spoken words is freedom indeed! Imagine the liberty of not needing to worry about someone discovering we broke a confidence or talked unkindly behind her back. God's way is always the path to freedom—powerful freedom.

It is foolish to spread a net where any bird
can see it, but they set an ambush to kill
themselves; they attack their own lives.

Proverbs 1:17–18

No sin, no matter how momentarily
pleasurable, comforting, or habitual is
worth missing what God has for us. Sin
can undoubtedly cost us our earthly destinies—yes, even the sin of our mouths.
No matter how stubborn the tongue or
how habitual our problem, God can make
it a vessel of honor and power.

But lasting change demands prayer
and attentive determination, because
bad habits are not easily broken. The
dividends, however, are huge. Daily de-
pendency on God develops unmatched
intimacy, and a clean mouth unplugs a
primary pipe of divine power.

When the Spirit of truth comes, He will
guide you into all the truth. . . . He will
also declare to you what is to come.

John 16:13

When you and I received Christ, the
Spirit of God took up immediate residency inside of us as our able Counselor and our blessed Reminder—not
to provoke deeply embedded, traumatic
memories but to quicken the memory of
God's faithful provision and His revealed
presence along the way.

So ask the Holy Spirit to remind you
of the works of Jesus throughout your
life: His presence, His activity, and many
of the things He has taught and revealed
to you. Like a river spilling into the sea,
actively remembering God in our past
spills into believing God for our future.

Clean out the old yeast so that you may be a new batch, since you are unleavened. For Christ our Passover has been sacrificed.

1 Corinthians 5:7

Many of you remember *The Scarlet Letter*, the novel that wardrobed its protagonist in a stigma or sign of reproach. But "A" is not the only letter a person can feel she is wearing. Some of us have looked like we spilled alphabet soup on our sweaters.

Beloved, if you are wearing any kind of reproach from your past—especially if victimization has placed a letter there that never belonged on you—may God remind you of the cross of Christ and memorialize the victory it brought you. Let Him cut that old piece of fabric from your life, roll it in the blood of Jesus, and cast it away forever.

JUNE

His mercies never end.
They are new every morning;
great is Your faithfulness!
Lamentations 3:22–23

God likes order. He likes repetition. A God of fundamentals, He brings up the sun every morning and the moon every evening. Still, I sometimes feel like the phrases I habitually use in prayer and the topics I'm most burdened to teach are surely getting old to God.

In reality, as long as He sees a genuine heart, He never gets tired of some of the same old words and practices that flow from it. God's mercies have existed throughout all of eternity, yet Scripture tells us they are new every morning. A new day with all its fresh challenges gives an old practice new life.

The LORD answered Moses,
"I will do this very thing you have asked,
for you have found favor in My sight."
Exodus 33:17

Moses' encounter with God in this scene from Exodus 33 is unmatched in Scripture. Moses placed his request before God, "Please let me see Your glory," and the Lord said, "I will cause all My goodness to pass in front of you" (verses 18–19). Moses became an eyewitness to the glory of God!

But why did he get to experience such a thing? Maybe because he had guts enough to ask. God glories in big prayers from people who have a big God. If, like Moses, our chief desire is for God to show His glory, God may delight in giving us our own special glimpse in the process.

Don't do that! I am a fellow slave
with you and your brothers who have the
testimony about Jesus. Worship God.
Revelation 19:10

If you become a person who makes a lifestyle of believing God, you will become
bolder in your love for others and what
you're willing to believe God for in their
lives. Your fruit is going to start showing,
and so is the power of your prayer life.

But along the way, people around you
are liable to start holding you responsible
for God's actions. Trust me, I've been
there. Scripture has a good name for what
some people try to make of those who
live with active faith: false christs. People
are so desperate to find Christ, they will-
ingly manufacture Him out of a mortal
with any vague resemblance. Be wary.

We are His creation—created in Christ
Jesus for good works, which God prepared
ahead of time that we should walk in them.
Ephesians 2:10

If you can't imagine God ever delivering you from the corruption of your evil desires and bringing forth a great harvest through your life, you've bought into the lie that God's promises don't apply to you. Beloved, they do!

God knew you before you were formed in your mother's womb and planned good works for you that would bring forth much fruit. According to Acts 17:26, He even determined the times and places set for you to live on planet Earth most conducive to your personalized harvests. You don't have to cooperate, but God's power is there when you do.

I pray that the eyes of your heart
may be enlightened so you may know
what is the hope of His calling.
Ephesians 1:18

Our glorious inheritance in Christ is not
meant for heaven alone. The primary
context of Ephesians 1 is the impact of
our heavenly inheritance on our earthly
existence.

But don't miss the word "hope" in the
verse above. Nothing about your calling
or mine is compulsory. God is going to
accomplish His agenda regarding heaven
and earth no matter what you and I do,
but we get to decide whether we're going
to be part of His process in our generation. Our callings remain a hope until we
allow the eyes of our hearts to be enlightened and choose to accept them.

Show me your faith
without works, and I will show
you faith from my works.

James 2:18

When I use the phrase "believing God," you can think of it interchangeably with having faith in God. I prefer the former expression because it has a far stronger implication of action. Faith is not just something you have. Faith is something you do. It can turn a noun into a verb quicker than you can say, "See Spot run."

Picture the page from an old first-grade primer. Spot wasn't *about* to run, future tense. Nor was he in a past-tense heap of exhaustion by his water bowl. "See Spot run" inferred he could presently be caught in the act of running. We want a present-tense faith!

I also say to you that you are Peter, and on
this rock I will build My church, and the
forces of Hades will not overpower it.
Matthew 16:18

Just a few verses after Jesus proclaimed
Peter's future place of authority by saying,
"I will give you the keys of the kingdom
of heaven" (verse 19), Peter rebuked Him
for having the audacity to suggest that
He would "suffer many things from the
elders, chief priests, and scribes" (verse
21). Had Peter had his way, he would have
bound the cross and unknowingly loosed
the world from any hope of salvation.

God doesn't sit upon His throne
saying, "Oops, I wouldn't have done that,
but now that you have, I guess I'll go with
it." Remember, God doesn't work for us;
we work for God.

Whatever you bind on earth is already
bound in heaven, and whatever you loose on
earth is already loosed in heaven.
Matthew 16:19

God has invited us to participate in kingdom affairs and, yes, even in kingdom
authority under the rule of His righteous
will. He extends staggering power to
those willing to think with the mind of
Christ rather than the mind of man. God
would also empower His children to
bind untold evils and strongholds if we'd
believe Him and cooperate with Him.
Talk about abundant life!

God is looking for stewards who are
willing to bind their own unbelief in the
mighty name of Jesus and loose a fresh
anointing of faith onto the topsoil of
earth. Are you game?

It is necessary to pass
through many troubles on our way
into the kingdom of God.

Acts 14:22

Many of the miracles we seek are toward the further avoidance of difficulty, pain, or suffering. Nothing is wrong with that. We have a blessed biblical precedent to ask repeatedly for thorns to be removed before we accept them as God's sovereign appointment for a greater work.

But we always need to remember: Suffering has an undeniable role in the New Testament and under the new covenant. Recognizing the role of suffering helps us understand a little more readily why God is able to perform a miracle He may not choose to perform. It's a matter of His priorities.

What does the Scripture say?
"Abraham believed God, and it was
credited to him for righteousness."
Romans 4:3

The fourth chapter of Romans frames one of my favorite revelations in all of Scripture—the fact that every time we believe God, He credits it to our account as righteousness.

The most obvious assumption is that God would credit our *righteous acts* as righteousness, but the prophet Isaiah penned the disclaimer that "all our righteous acts are like filthy rags" (Isa. 64:6 NIV).

So it's clear that nothing good can come from our good works. God insists in Scripture that believing Him is what He credits to our account as righteousness. And He gets to make the rules.

He said to them,
"Why are you fearful?
Do you still have no faith?"
Mark 4:40

A friend and I had been driving through Yellowstone National Park for some time when she looked anxiously ahead and asked, "How much longer till we see Old Yeller?" I laughed until I nearly ran off the road into a buffalo herd. "Old *Yeller?* You mean Old *Faithful?*"

Where I come from, you see, "yeller" means "cowardly." So her *faux pax* made a perfect application in my head for what believing God really means. When all is said and done, you and I will be either Old Faithful or Old Yeller, but we will never be both. One will always elbow out the other.

My servant Jacob, do not be afraid, and
do not be discouraged, Israel, for without
fail I will save you from far away.
Jeremiah 46:27

Though I couldn't have articulated it at
the time, for years my deepest fear was
that I was a weakling, powerless to temptation, and that I—the victim—would
break under pressure every time.

I was a victim, all right—a victim to
my own erroneous belief system. Satan
quickly detected my fears and preyed on
them, doing everything he could to con-
firm what I believed.

Once again we see a huge reason why
we must believe we are who God says we
are and that we can do all things through
Christ. Satan will always discourage and
demoralize us if we don't.

Take your sandals off your
feet, for the place where you are
standing is holy ground.
Exodus 3:5

Faith is never the denial of reality; it is belief in a greater reality. In other words, the truth may be that you are presently surrounded by terrifying or terribly discouraging circumstances. But the reason why you don't have to buckle to fear and discouragement is the presence of God in the middle of your circumstances.

So call upon Him to step His One and Only shoes onto your territory. This place—this circumstance—is now holy because God stands on it with you. You don't have to fill His shoes, Dear One. Take off your sandals and walk barefoot in His wake.

The LORD says . . . "Do not fear,
for I have redeemed you; I have called
you by your name; you are Mine."
Isaiah 43:1

Failure takes all sorts of forms and hits all sorts of unsuspecting, sincere followers of Jesus Christ. We don't have to sin grievously to feel like we've failed. Sometimes all it takes is feeling like we've proved ineffective and untalented too many times to try again.

What about you? Do you feel you've failed God in some way? Are you too scared or discouraged to try serving God again? Have you allowed Satan to demoralize you by preying on your fear that you are nothing but a failure? Then hear these words: God will not fail you! Grab onto Him with everything you have.

The Lord GOD has given Me the tongue
of those who are instructed to know how
to sustain the weary with a word.

Isaiah 50:4

Having God's Word upon our tongues
certainly means more than just quoting
Bible verses. It doesn't always externalize through exact Scripture recitation.
It often takes the form of simple godly
conversation.

Encouragement, instruction, exhortation, counsel, and yes, even at times the
issue of an appropriate rebuke are a few
ways God's Word upon our tongues can
accomplish and achieve.

Oh, the positive power of having
an instructed tongue! How many weary
people do we encounter day after day
who could use a sustaining word.

A ruler can be persuaded
through patience, and a gentle
tongue can break a bone.
Proverbs 25:15

You may wonder, "Aren't actions more powerful than words?" Without a doubt, we externalize the internal works of the Spirit through action as well. Speech without action is all talk and no walk.

But I'm talking about a different practice and purpose: the specific power that is released when we "believe and therefore speak" (2 Cor. 4:13).

Being created in the image of our omnipotent God, our spoken words are potent. Speaking what we believe—even from ourselves *to* ourselves—is like inviting our souls to a pep rally. Vocalized words stir enthusiasm.

The reflections of the heart
belong to man, but the answer of
the tongue is from the LORD.
Proverbs 16:1

We can't talk about the God-endorsed power of words without specifying the words of prayer. Every time we make a petition to God, we are using words that have elements of accomplishing and achieving power, even if we pray silently.

I have found, however, that I sense more power in prayer when I speak them out loud. Please understand, the difference rests in me rather than God. He hears and receives petitions of any kind that are prayed in Jesus' name. But I tend to be a lot gutsier in my vocalized prayers because hearing them with my own ears ignites my heart and mind all the more.

A good man produces good things from his storeroom of good, and an evil man produces evil things from his storeroom of evil.

Matthew 12:35

The tongue's potential to wreak havoc is staggering, yet so is the potential to reap the stuff of heaven on the stuff of earth. Therefore, we can rest assured God and Satan are both vying for authority over our mouths.

Nothing is a greater threat to the enemy than a believer with the Word of God living and active upon her tongue, readily applied to any situation, speaking what she knows to be true.

If no part of the body is harder to submit to godly authority than the tongue, what could possess more power to reap benefit than one He controls?

We must not get tired of doing
good, for we will reap at the proper
time if we don't give up.
Galatians 6:9

Beloved, God is not tired. Nor is God
tired of you. He delights in your atten-
tions even when you practice them much
like you did yesterday. He waits for you
to awaken each morning, and He antici-
pates His time with you.

Somehow in the Lord's self-existent
essence and omniscience, His foreknowledge does not cheat Him of reactive
emotion. He laughs when you delight
Him. He listens when you speak to Him.
He honors you when you persevere with
Him. In all the changes He is making
within you and me, He rejoices in the
few things that call for blessed sameness.

At the beginning of your petitions
an answer went out, and I have come to
give it, for you are treasured by God.
Daniel 9:23

God can delight in our courage to pray big prayers without necessarily giving us what we ask. Said another way, God can say yes to the *heart* of our prayer without saying yes to the request of our prayer. He will approve of the petitioner even when, for whatever reason, He can't approve the petition.

I'm convinced God is more pleased when we believe Him enough to ask for a hundred huge things (though they may be granted in part) than to believe Him for a few and get everything we asked. We all err in many ways. Let us err on the side of faith.

No, in all these things
we are more than victorious
through Him who loved us.
Romans 8:37

One way we can measure our belief system's effectiveness is to examine how consistently our biblical position as "more than conquerors" is fleshed out in our reality.

The children of Israel showed they were God's conquerors on earth by conquering. Victory assumes a counterpart defeat. We will never take our places as "more than overcomers" with nothing to overcome. We will never be victors without opponents. God gave the Israelites the Promised Land but told them they'd have to take what was theirs in fierce battle. We should expect no less today.

I am sure of this, that He who started a good
work in you will carry it on to completion
until the day of Christ Jesus.
Philippians 1:6

Our glorious walk with God began with
an act of faith that brought us into relationship with Jesus Christ as our Savior,
but it doesn't end there. *Having believed* in
Christ, we've been called to continue believing all that He came to do and say.

Quite tragically, some who have believed *in* Christ have believed little *of* Him
since. But He who began a good work in
us has far more He wants to accomplish.
God is calling you and me to leave the life
of passivity bred by a past-tense view of
faith and get caught in the act of present-
active-participle believing. Nothing in
life could be more exhilarating.

How great is Your goodness that You
have stored up for those who fear You and
accomplished in the sight of everyone.

Psalm 31:19

Why in the world would God give *carte
blanche* permission to human flesh and
blood to bind and loose whatever he (the
believer) interpreted was wrong or right?
If God had given me my way, I would
have bound and loosed three or four hus-
bands by the time I was twenty-five. His
desire is to see believers bind and loose
what He wants for them.

God has made so much available to
us. He foreordained a perfect plan for
each of our lives and has stored up immeasurable blessing that He longs for His
children to loose by faith. It's time we did
so by discovering more of who He is.

Now to Him who is able to do above and beyond all that we ask or think . . . to Him be glory in the church and in Christ Jesus.
Ephesians 3:20–21

New Testament Scripture stacks up far too much evidence for us to claim that suffering is never within the plan of our sovereign God, whether through His perfect or permissive will.

Does this discourage me from asking and believing God for miracles? Hardly! And I'll tell you why. Knowing the truth about God, His unceasing ability to perform miracles, and the truth about the undeniable role of suffering only frees me up to believe Him more. I used to treat a miracle as a last hope. But now, if I don't receive it, I assume God has a more inward agenda.

There is no one like You,
and there is no God besides You,
as all we have heard confirms.

2 Samuel 7:22

One of the things that keeps us from getting out there and believing God is being scared half to death that He won't come through for us, won't dignify us with a yes, and ultimately won't prove faithful in the end. Or that we'll prove to be failures at having enough belief for Him to bless with a miracle.

If I'm convinced that God really loves me and has certain priorities for me that may take precedence at times, then I am "safe" to walk by faith. I am freed to know that my God is huge and my God is able and that if I don't get what I asked, if I'll cooperate, I'll get something bigger.

I am like a flourishing olive tree
in the house of God; I trust in God's
faithful love forever and ever.

Psalm 52:8

I believe God can do anything His Word says He can. So if He chooses not to, I don't have to assume He doesn't like me, doesn't answer my prayers, hardly knows I'm alive, isn't willing to do it, or is still punishing me for that sin in my past—or that I don't have enough faith and am just making a fool of myself. Instead, I get to know that a greater yes is in progress, and I can count on the bigger miracle.

Beloved, we are safe with God—free to believe He is who He says He is and can do what He says He can. Neither His dignity nor ours is at stake. We are safe with Him because we *are* His priority.

What should we say then?
Should we continue in sin in order
that grace may multiply?
Romans 6:1

To many, the fact that God has declared us holy and righteous before Him by means of Christ's substitutionary death gives us license to sin. But we would be severely mistaken to rationalize God's grace and forgiveness into permission to act like pagans.

Those who presently and actively believe God are prompted to make wiser and healthier decisions. Authentic faith cannot help but act. If we really believe what the Word says about God and about us, our decisions and behaviors will reflect it. How we behave overwhelmingly flows from what we deeply believe.

How happy those whose lawless acts are forgiven! ... How happy the man whom the Lord will never charge with sin!

Romans 4:7–8

These verses must have meant as much to Paul with his sinful past as they mean to me. I suppose all of us with histories of heinous sin cling to any affirmation that God really can forgive and use those with terrible pasts.

In the Greek, the word translated "never" is a double negative. So we might read the passage like this: "How happy the man whom the Lord will 'no, never' charge with sin." The word "charge" is an accounting term, the same word used in Romans 4:3. All that time I thought God was counting my sins, and He was counting my faith as righteousness instead.

She said to herself,
"If I can just touch His robe,
I'll be made well!"
Matthew 9:21

Perhaps like me, you have grievously failed God in the past. Perhaps like me, your prior confidence was unknowingly in your own ability and determination to stay on track.

Then cast yourself today entirely upon *His* ability to succeed and not yours. Blind yourself to all ambition except to please Him. Walk in the shadow of the Almighty. Grab onto the hem of His garment and find the healing and grace to go where He leads. In that place you will be equipped to do the impossible. There you can do all things through Christ who strengthens you.

Shout to God with a jubilant cry.
For the LORD Most High is awe-inspiring,
a great King over all the earth.
Psalm 47:1–2

God has so much for you, Dear One. And yes, seasons will come when He requires so much from you that you feel like you can't bear it.

You do have a choice. You don't have to do it His way. You can choose bitterness, resentment, carnality, or mediocrity. Or you can go for it—with everything you've got. You can experience the unmatched exhilaration of partnering in divine triumph.

The stakes are high. The cost is steep. But I'll promise you this: there is no high like the Most High. Don't you dare miss it for the world.

JULY

Pray to your Father who is
in secret. And your Father who sees
in secret will reward you.
Matthew 6:6

Anytime you put forth the time and attention that a book like this requires—
and you exercise the faith to apply what
you learn—you will be rewarded. God is
the giver of all good gifts. He wants us to
be men and women He can bless.

God's pleasure is the end; our faith
is the means. We are invited to believe
in God. The eye-opening news may be
that we can also believe Him for reward,
as long as our desire for reward doesn't
exceed our desire for Him personally.
Sooner or later, your God-seeking faith
will be rewarded. You will never out-
spend God.

If we know that He hears whatever
we ask, we know that we have what
we have asked Him for.
1 John 5:15

Don't get discouraged if you don't have
or don't presently practice everything
God desires of you. Pray for what you
lack! When you pray God's will, you will
receive what you ask!

Pray for a heart and mind that diligently seeks Him. Then begin walking in
faith, as one who already possesses what
she has asked. Start seeking God through
His Word and spending time in prayer,
at the same time asking Him for a hunger
and thirst to seek Him diligently. He will
develop in you what you are seeking. He
will give you everything you need for living in faith and belief!

How long will you hesitate between
two opinions? If Yahweh is God, follow
Him. But if Baal, follow him.
1 Kings 18:21

Sometimes our problem with God is that
we don't like the rules. I can remember
trying to hang on to both God and my
idols. As my grandmother would say, I
wanted to have my cake and eat it too.
Have you tried that approach?

I felt as if God spoke to my heart and
said, "Child, My precepts are from everlasting to everlasting. You're not going to
be the one for whom the rules change.
Repent of your arrogance and lay those
idols down." The requirement of faith
before we see certain acts of God is one
way He forces our engagement with Him
in an active relationship.

Jesus replied to her,
"Woman, your faith is great.
Let it be done for you as you want."
Matthew 15:28

Why do you think God is sometimes willing to reveal Himself dramatically even when we're not actively believing Him? Though God may have countless reasons, the most probable cause is to encourage belief. He graciously reminds us that He can . . . and still does.

But if we persist in our stubborn unbelief after such merciful revelation, we can probably expect to see less and less activity of God. He certainly makes exceptions, but He primarily wants our faith. That means the more we believe God, the more we are likely to see and experience His intervening power.

Because of laziness the roof
caves in, and because of negligent
hands the house leaks.
Ecclesiastes 10:18

Our resistance to faith is most commonly caused by spiritual laziness and lethargy. Believing God can really be hard work at times! But even when external evidences scream to the contrary, we have to be able to exert volitional muscle. Deciding to believe God's Word over our circumstances can be a tremendous exercise of the will.

Let me just go ahead and say it: the great adventure of faith is not for the languid. But if He can raise the dead, He can surely enliven the lazy! We have been called to a present-active-participle walk of faith, not a park 'n' ride.

I have promised you in marriage
to one husband—to present
a pure virgin to Christ.
2 Corinthians 11:2

For much of my life I was a habitual sinner, cycling in and out of defeat. I hated myself and the choices I continued to make, but I was powerless to stop.

To the praise, glory, and honor of my wonderful God, I have been free from this cycle of defeat for years. Do you know how? I chose to believe God. He said I was forgiven. That I was beautiful to Him. That He had a purpose for my life. That I was a new woman—a virgin, no less. I chose to believe Him one day at a time, and that's how God broke the cycle. We have no hope of authentic righteousness without it.

The Spirit is the One who gives life. The flesh doesn't help at all. The words that I have spoken to you are spirit and are life.

John 6:63

I'm pretty convinced at this point that I want to live my life believing God. Too much is at stake, and too much adventure stands to be missed. If faith pleases God and invites such incomparable divine intervention in my life, I want to exercise it lavishly, don't you?

But like much of what God asks from us, we have to receive it from Him before we can offer it back. Even our initial faith to believe Christ for salvation came through the work and conviction of the Holy Spirit. We can't just manufacture faith from what the Scripture calls our "natural man." Faith is ours from God.

When the Counselor comes . . .
the Spirit of truth who proceeds from
the Father—He will testify about Me.
John 15:26

As New Testament believers, the Holy Spirit comes to dwell in us when we receive Christ as our personal Savior, and He brings His personality with Him. When we are deliberately yielded to the Holy Spirit's authority, His personality fills us and eclipses our own.

You see, the more we are filled with the Spirit, the more faith we can possess. Because the Holy Spirit is one with the Father and the Son, He always believes God. So when He fills us, our fleshly faithlessness yields to His belief system, and we get to possess and exercise it as our own.

You see that faith was active
together with his works, and by
works, faith was perfected.
James 2:22

I used to think of faith as believing God,
while I tended to imagine faithfulness
as obediently serving God and keeping
His commands. Though faith certainly
encompasses serving and obeying God, I
am opening my spiritual eyes to the fact
that faith is the root of all faithfulness to
God.

In fact, we might say that ultimately,
faithfulness—serving and obeying God—
is the outward expression of an inward
fullness of faith. With a little different
twist on the meaning, we can say it the
way we've said it before: *faith works*. It lives
itself out in our faithful behavior.

He would feed Israel with
the best wheat. "I would satisfy you
with honey from the rock."
Psalm 81:16

Thank goodness, our faith in God keeps developing, maturing and growing as we continue to walk with Him. I believe the more we practice faith, the more faith we'll have to practice. Those who continually feed on God's faithfulness are far more likely to have a ready supply when the challenge arises, because it abides in them.

I love the idea of feeding on God's faithfulness. Might we say, in fact, that the more we feed on God's faithfulness, the fatter of faith we become? How's that for a diet reversal? I'm thrilled to know we can binge on God without guilt.

Endurance must do its complete
work, so that you may be mature and
complete, lacking nothing.

James 1:4

Faith unchallenged is faith stifled. How
could we ever grow in our faith and get
a fresh belief in our systems if we were
smugly unconvinced that we could use
some alteration? We must be willing to
have our faith challenged if we want to
give it a little fresh air to grow in.

Some of our belief systems haven't
changed in so long, they have cobwebs.
Believers who know what they want to
believe and refuse to be challenged may
have a *stand* of faith, but they may not
have a *walk* of faith. You and I don't want
to get stagnant on our journey of belief.
We want to keep moving with our God!

They welcomed the message with
eagerness and examined the Scriptures
daily to see if these things were so.

Acts 17:11

If we are going to believe God, our plumb
line for measuring the accuracy of biblical concepts must be the Bible itself, not
what we've seen or heard. We must also
be willing for God to broaden our biblical concepts of who He is and what He
can do.

Our human tendency is to affirm
and reaffirm spiritually and biblically
what we already believe rather than to
search and consider the whole counsel
of the Word. But wherever our trained
belief systems lack biblical support, we
must have enough courage to believe
what God says over what people say.

This extraordinary knowledge
is beyond me. It is lofty;
I am unable to reach it.
Psalm 139:6

Some of our favorite teachers may have
helped us package our faith in neat little
boxes and even handed us the wrapping
paper and bows, as if we need not know
another thing. We think we've got God
in those boxes, but we don't. God doesn't
fit in boxes.

However high, wide, long, or deep
your faith may grow through the years,
always leave an ellipsis at every point
of your spiritual compass. Anything at-
tainable by human understanding is a
mere shadow of the reality. Every time
you grasp a new concept about God, try
thinking, "He's this . . . and more."

They will not labor without success or
bear children destined for disaster, for they
will be a people blessed by the LORD.
Isaiah 65:23

The last thing I'm trying to encourage a
thinking person to do is to surrender to a
life of nothing but stark, blind faith. The
reason I don't believe that aliens live on
Mars is that we've never seen evidence
to suggest they do. If I had evidence, I'd
be far more inclined to believe, even if I
never saw them with my own eyes.

Much more importantly, I wouldn't
encourage anyone to believe in a God of
heaven if we had no evidence to support
that He exists as the Bible says He does.
The reason I teach belief in God is that,
again and again, I have found Him to be
astoundingly believable.

Let no one deceive you with empty
arguments, for because of these things God's
wrath is coming on the disobedient.
Ephesians 5:6

To be sure, believers should seek to be
well educated about current events and
intellectual trends, but we need not feel
quite so responsible to defend God.
While the waves of godless intellectual-
ism rise and fall and the trends set the
tides, you and I are better off watching
from the nearest solid Rock.

I have a tremendous respect for
theological apologists. Their arguments
strengthen my faith. But most of us are
not called to prove unbelievers intellec-
tually wrong. God will tend to that, all in
a matter of time. He knows the defiant
will end up making fools of themselves.

He forgives all your sin;
He heals all your diseases.
He redeems your life from the Pit.
Psalm 103:3–4

One definition of the word "heals" in the verse above is "to mend by stitching." I love the thought expressed in that. A seamstress cannot mend a fabric that she doesn't hold in her hands. Likewise, God cradles us in His careful hands as He stitches our broken pieces back together again, forming a new and far more beautiful garment.

The word picture of stitching also suggests "process" to me. Almost all the healing works God has accomplished in my life have been processes, stitch-by-stitch, so that I would learn to appreciate being continually in His hands.

I will bring you health and will heal you
of your wounds . . . for they call you The
Outcast, the Zion no one cares about.
Jeremiah 30:17

I wonder whether the way God heals
may vary according to His objective. If
the primary objective is to show His supremacy, for example, perhaps He might
choose to heal instantaneously. If His
primary objective is to teach sufficiency
in Him or to mature and build faith, I
wonder whether He heals through the
stitch-by-stitch method.

Remember, God is far more inter-
ested in our knowing the Healer than He
is in the healing. God can be vastly glorified through either objective, whether in
showing His supremacy or showing His
sufficiency.

Pray for one another, so that you
may be healed. The intense prayer of
the righteous is very powerful.

James 5:16

Dear One, we can't let our fear that God
may not affirmatively answer our every
prayer keep us from praying! Great men
like Moses and Elijah were tremendously
used by God, but neither got everything
he asked. You will be hard pressed to find
anyone in Scripture who did—including
Christ! Check out what happened in the
garden of Gethsemane.

What if these men of God hadn't
asked for anything because they couldn't
have everything? Can you imagine the
loss? As we faithfully and fervently pray,
we will experience many astounding and
affirmative answers. Pray on, Beloved!

> John heard in prison what the
> Messiah was doing . . . and asked Him,
> "Are You the One who is to come?"
> Matthew 11:2–3

Imagine John's predicament. If he had been wrong about Jesus, he had either sacrificed all for nothing or missed the real Messiah. And if he had been right? Then Jesus had the power to free him from prison and death and simply wasn't using it. Have you ever had a time when none of your obvious multiple-choice answers were good options?

All of us called to faith will have this knife-sharp experience at some point. Few of us will escape a painful opportunity to be offended with Christ. It is part of the believer's life test, but be sure our Teacher gives no accidental exams.

My flesh and my heart may fail,
but God is the strength of my heart,
my portion forever.
Psalm 73:26

At times we'll be tempted to think, "If Christ is who He says He is, and can do what He says He can do, and I am His beloved, why isn't He coming through for me?" Is it our insignificance? Is He too busy to notice? Is the situation simply not critical to the overall plan?

I'd go so far as to say that the deeper we have loved God, the deeper the potential for devastation when He doesn't intervene as we know He can. But He knows our hearts and understands our confusion. Blessed are we when we could easily be offended yet choose with every shred of tattered faith not to be.

He is the image of the invisible God, the firstborn over all creation. . . . He is before all things, and by Him all things hold together.

Colossians 1:15, 17

Not only is Christ responsible for creating the heavens and the earth, but the fact that each still operates with its environment is His doing as well. He also created the human body, more "fearfully and wonderfully" than any other work.

When you calculate the thousands of functions simultaneously occurring within the human body, the wonder that any of us are well far exceeds the perplexity that any of us are ill. Therefore, it is likely that each one of us has experienced God's miraculous healing any number of times without knowing it—every day that our fragile tents of flesh hold together.

If you do right, won't you be
accepted? But if you do not do right,
sin is crouching at the door.
Genesis 4:7

Don't miss God's intimation in this verse that Cain knew what was right; he simply didn't do it. Cain's offering represents every time a believer knows what God wants but refuses to give it. We often give Him other things, as if He won't notice. We give more in other areas but we doggedly withhold the one thing we know He wants. And sin crouches at our door.

What made Abel's offering more acceptable? I have a feeling he didn't know the answer himself. God had obviously made clear to both Cain and Abel that He wanted a sacrificial offering, and Abel just presented it . . . by faith.

Enoch was taken away so that he
did not experience death. . . . He was
approved, having pleased God.

Hebrews 11:5

I'd like to suggest that God's testimony
on the life of Enoch represents the ultimate commendation. Short and sweet:
he "pleased God."

You and I know that the entire purpose of our existence is to please God.
Therefore, Enoch crossed the finish line,
not with a perfect life, but with a perfect
testimony.

Not bad. In fact, I wouldn't mind the
same one, would you? We don't have to
be covetous to want it, because we don't
have to take away from another soul's
testimony to have it. Each of us has our
own opportunity to please God.

What no eye has seen and
no ear has heard . . . is what God has
prepared for those who love Him.

1 Corinthians 2:9

Our perceptions have been so distorted by our world system, we fear that God's path may be smooth and respectable but it's sure to be boring. Does that sound anything at all like the life described for us in 1 Corinthians 2:9?

The only way we will have an earthly experience with God that is more than eyes have seen, ears have heard, and minds have ever imagined is to walk with Him. When we choose to walk with Him rather than off the path for handfuls of other options, we find His perfect will for our lives. Instead of finding Less-Than Land, we find our Promised Land.

Wisdom is the focus of the
perceptive, but a fool's eyes roam
to the ends of the earth.

Proverbs 17:24

I have discovered that if Satan can't get to me with destruction, he will try distraction. Each of us could name a dozen different things we'd really like to do with our lives . . . sometimes all in the same day.

We have only one turn on this green earth. We will never get to do this again. We cannot do a hundred things to the glory of God, but we can certainly do a few. What you and I need to do is focus. Day in and day out. Eyes on the goal. We are desperate for simplicity in our frenzied lives. We need those hundred things to narrow down to one.

I make every effort to take
hold of it because I also have been
taken hold of by Christ Jesus.
Philippians 3:12

God created us. He knows what satisfies
our souls and fulfills us. He could grant
us victory and maturity without an ounce
of participation, but He created us to be
most satisfied by apprehending through
diligent pursuit.

Our salvation is a free gift of grace
that demanded the work of Jesus alone.
God made sure, however, that much of
our fulfillment would involve the glorious pursuit of God and His goals so our
souls would be filled and thrilled in the
constant discoveries. God is sovereign,
Dear One. And when all is said and done,
He knows what will thrill us the most.

First, be aware of this:
scoffers will come in the last days to
scoff, following their own lusts.

2 Peter 3:3

It is merely a fact of life that those who actively believe God in every generation are liable to be scoffed at. So we may as well be prepared in advance for others—sometimes other Christians—to ridicule us or think we are uneducated and unsophisticated to believe that God's Word applies to us today. Sometimes we may even be tempted to wonder whether we're wrong ourselves.

But, Beloved, God is right. And you can rest assured that He will prove it once again, sooner or later. Peer pressure is a powerful faith deterrent. Don't let it cheat you of your promised land.

So those who have faith
are blessed with Abraham,
who had faith.
Galatians 3:9

The fact that God esteemed Abraham so highly and spoke of him so often encourages me beyond words, because not only does Abraham have a history of faith, but his record also bears the marks of some serious bouts with doubt and remarkably foolish decisions. So does mine.

Each of us sitting here today are alive and kicking. And no matter what our track record of doubt and foolishness has been in the past, we can still give God the opportunity to testify to our faith. We still have today to believe God. Let's not put it off until tomorrow. Failure isn't terminal, Dear One. Faithlessness is.

Yes, LORD, we wait for You in the
path of Your judgments. Our desire
is for Your name and renown.
Isaiah 26:8

Time can test almost anything and undoubtedly anyone. Sometimes when we
obey God and go where we believe He is
sending us, we're not altogether certain
what we expected, but after a while we
ascertain, "This certainly can't be it." In
fact, obeying God can initially seem to
get us into a bigger mess than we left.

It can make you think, "I must be an
alien here." But actually, that may be your
first indication you're in the right place.
We can be in the bull's-eye of God's will
for our lives even when things make utterly no sense. Sometimes we just to wait
on that ugly, five-letter word: "later."

He was looking forward to the city
that has foundations, whose architect
and builder is God.

Hebrews 11:10

Time by itself does nothing but grow us old. It's what we *do* with time that makes all the difference. We often say, "Time heals," yet I've known just as many that time embittered. Only God heals. Only God restores. Only God effectively prepares, teaches, equips, and matures. But you can count on Him to use the test tube of time in which to accomplish it.

We tend to argue, "God, why are You waiting so long? I don't have much time here!" We forget that God sees the big picture, and that His primary objective for us on earth is to prepare us for a city of which He is architect and builder.

Instead, he is under
guardians and stewards until
the time set by his father.
Galatians 4:2

Sometimes God waits until we have a little maturity before He places more important trusts in our hands. Beloved, the world will not stop and our true God-ordained ministries will not end when we take the time to let God make us healthier and better equipped.

When the height of a ministry outgrows its depth, it will inevitably come tumbling down. So we are wise when we focus on the depth alone and leave the length, breadth, and height to Him. As long as the latter dimensions are what matter most to us, we are not ready to build what lasts.

AUGUST

What a wretched man I am!
Who will rescue me from
this body of death?
Romans 7:24

I am so glad God didn't limit Holy Writ
to high and lofty subjects. From the birth
of family life, He revealed how entangled
and awry our human natures can grow in
relationship to one another.

In fact, I have yet to find the story
of a fully healthy and functional family
in the Word of God. He graciously made
sure we'd know that in things pertaining
to the sons of earth, abnormal is more
normal than normal. That doesn't mean
we should surrender to dysfunction. It
just means we don't have to hang our
heads as we surrender and let Him sort
out our tangled mess.

We have sworn an oath to them
by the LORD, the God of Israel,
and now we cannot touch them.

Joshua 9:19

If an ancient Hebrew invoked the name of the Lord God in a vow, he believed God alone had the power to break it. Because the Israelites understood Him to be a covenant God and knew that He was faithful, they more readily assumed that the vow was utterly binding.

I am convicted by how thoughtlessly I often petition something "in the name of Jesus" without really seeking the heart and will of God in the matter. We need to be careful what we pray. Sometimes our hasty, popcorn prayers reveal a lack of conviction in the true power of the name of Jesus.

Isaac answered Esau: "Look,
I have made him a master over you. . . .
What then can I do for you, my son?"
Genesis 27:37

When Isaac grew old and the time came
to pass on the family blessing, he chose
to respect God's sovereignty even though
he'd been deceived. I believe Isaac knew
God well enough to discern when more
might be at work than met the eye.

We view faith primarily from the
standpoint of action. We believe, therefore we act. But Isaac, Esau, and Jacob's
experience teaches us a harder dimension: what to do when faith requires us
to do nothing while our human nature
screams to interfere. In these cases, we
believe, therefore we do *not* act. Wisdom
knows the difference between the two.

Peter and John answered them, "Whether it's right in the sight of God for us to listen to you rather than to God, you decide."

Acts 4:19

Misunderstandings can often result as we exercise enough faith to do what we're convinced is God's will. Sometimes those misunderstandings can involve people whose opinions are very important to us. But if we are convinced that God has willed the action, let's go the extra faith mile and believe that God will handle the consequences.

Years ago He taught me a principle I've never forgotten: the consequences of our humble obedience are His problem, not ours. We don't want to *make* anyone want to withhold blessing, but we must obey God either with it or without it.

The LORD then said to Moses,
"Write this down on a scroll as a reminder
and recite it to Joshua."
Exodus 17:14

At the time, young Joshua had no idea that before he was born, God had chosen him to lead the conquest of Canaan. He also had no idea that he was already in training. He was both a warrior and a worshiper long before he led the Israelites into the Promised Land.

But none of his training was wasted. Nor is ours, Dear One. If we try to skip our training and jump to the thrill of leveling the walls of Jericho, all the huffing and puffing in the world won't even blow the dust off our boots. We'll end up shouting, all right—but more than likely at one another.

By faith the walls of
Jericho fell down after being
encircled for seven days.
Hebrews 11:30

Imagine standing next to God as, with His outstretched arm, His index finger pointed out your own personal Jerichos. Hear Him say to you, "Child, would you please see this the way I do—not through your eyes, but through the eyes of faith?"

Today, pinpoint what this particular Jericho may be for you. Don't quickly assume. Keep in mind that we sometimes misdiagnose our own problems and fight the wrong foes. Ask God to give you insight into any Jericho that stands between you and your promised land. Then ask Him for the grace to follow Him there in triumphal procession.

By faith Rahab the prostitute
received the spies in peace and didn't
perish with those who disobeyed.
Hebrews 11:31

Any given day of the week, I think I love something different about God best of all. Today I love best of all what He's willing to do for a damsel in distress like Rahab. I am a hopeless romantic, and I fall in love with Him all over again every time I see this Prince Charming side of Him.

You won't find a fairy godmother in a single scene of the biblical account of Rahab the harlot. Her Cinderella story is not only PG-13 but also maybe a little farfetched. Of course, maybe that's what I love best of all about God. We've never gone so far that we can't be fetched.

Lying lips are detestable
to the LORD, but faithful people
are His delight.
Proverbs 12:22

Lies come in many forms, ranging from slight exaggerations and likely excuses to complete fabrications. Their primary motivations are self-protection and self-exaltation. Unfortunately, the tendency of the natural man toward deception is as deep and pulsing as the heart within us.

Because the mouth speaks from the overflow of the heart, an untreated heart will easily give way to a lying tongue. Each of us could regularly use a fresh work of healing and purification at the very source of our deception problem. The Lord desires "integrity in the inner self" (Ps. 51:6). We should too.

Do not let the oppressed
turn away in shame; let the poor
and needy praise Your name.
Psalm 74:21

If you struggle with an extremely habit-forming practice like profanity, please know that you can be extremely honest with God about it. I'd hate for you to know the habits God has empowered me to break. But openly dialoguing with Him about my strongholds and telling Him in advance when I felt that old, familiar setup for failure are the most vital practices God ever taught me.

I still don't hesitate to tell Him when I'm feeling weak or vulnerable to attack. I know I can talk to God without shame, expecting Him to come to my aid. You can too! He will never turn you away.

Then I said: "Woe is me, for I am ruined,
because I am a man of unclean lips and
live among a people of unclean lips."
Isaiah 6:5

God wants to send us into our world in His name. And our tongue is the instrument of His greatest potential use. Think of how many of Christ's New Testament commands involve our mouths.

We've been called to share Jesus with the lost and give our testimonies anytime we have the opportunity to tell another person of our hope. We've been called to pray. We've been called to disciple others, teaching God's Word and ways. We've been called to resist the devil as Christ did, with the spoken Word of God. We've even been called to speak to some mountains and tell them to move!

Blessed be the God and Father of our Lord Jesus Christ, who has blessed us with every spiritual blessing in the heavens, in Christ.

Ephesians 1:3

I want you to understand and celebrate today, Dear One, that God has used His powerful mouth to call you by name and speak blessing over you. Absorb this: God has been talking about you and over you. That's right. Behind your back.

Thank goodness, I have those who bless me with pure encouragement, as well as those who offer their gracious, loving correction. All of us could use a few others to speak good words over us. You and I can also become people who speak good words over others. If we do, can you even imagine how God will talk behind our backs then?

Be compassionate and humble, not paying
back evil for evil or insult for insult but,
on the contrary, giving a blessing.
1 Peter 3:8–9

Let's employ the day ahead as an opportunity for using our mouths to bless God.
Let's also ask Him to bring to our minds
anyone He wants us to bless.

Perhaps someone could even use the
blessing of our apology, especially if we
have used our words to wound them. I'm
not meaning to fill your heart with condemnation, but we want the day cleared
to start using our mouths with power and
blessing. Humbling ourselves and apologizing to someone we may have hurt is a
small price to pay. So if God brings anyone to mind, go forward in obedience,
knowing the harvest is ahead!

If anyone is in Christ, there is a
new creation; old things have passed away,
and look, new things have come.
2 Corinthians 5:17

The more thoroughly convinced we become that we are who God says we are, the more we will begin to *act* like who He says we are. Our daily lives demonstrate what we really believe about ourselves.

Most of us have bought a whole lot more of what others have said than we'd like to admit. Dear One, the time has come to believe God. The time has come for us to renounce the words others have spoken over us that don't line up with the truth of God's Word. And while we're at it, let's give others the same privilege we want for ourselves. They get to be who God says they are, too.

Just as the Lord has forgiven you,
so also you must forgive. Above all,
put on love—the perfect bond of unity.
Colossians 3:13–14

Perhaps the coming day would be a good time for you to find a private place where you can pray aloud. No matter how much the process temporarily stings, verbalize every statement contrary to God's Word that has wielded significant power over you. Tell God how the words hurt. And in Jesus' name, renounce every statement one by one. Then believe God to completely release you.

Thank Him that none of these injurious statements have further authority over you. And ask Him to empower you to forgive those who said them, in the same way He has forgiven you.

Can a woman forget her nursing child, or
lack compassion for the child of her womb?
Even if these forget, yet I will not forget you.
Isaiah 49:15

If God never forgets His children, what
does He mean when He says He remembers us? I'd like to suggest to you that for
God, "remembered" isn't the opposite of
"forget." The vast majority of references
to God's remembering also record a subsequent action or promise of action.

Beloved, we can be sure that God
never forgets His people. Almost every
time we see God "remembering" in the
Scripture, it means that He is about to
stretch forth His mighty arm and swing
into action. And when He stands, His
enemies are certain to scatter! God acts
on what He remembers.

I continually remember them and
have become depressed. Yet I call this
to mind, and therefore I have hope.
Lamentations 3:20–21

We may not be able to throw away our
difficult memories, but we can reframe
them against the backdrop of God's at-
tributes. We can also call on His ability to
change the course of our future, no matter the pattern of our past. He breaks the
strongholds of our negative meditations
when we reframe our old memories with
God in the picture.

Anytime we agree to see God accu-
rately in any portrait, all else is dwarfed
by and bows down in His presence. The
difficulty soon becomes little more than
a measuring stick by which we estimate
the size of a huge God.

I am deeply depressed;
therefore I remember You from the land
of Jordan and the peaks of Hermon.
Psalm 42:6

Beloved, both freedom and faith emerge from deliberate acts of the will to shift our focus from all that begs to differ to the great and glorious truth of the living God. Neither freedom nor faith is ever accidental. As we refocus on the God of our past and remember His goodness, we are far more inclined to believe Him in our present and future.

So be deliberate, Dear One, because God has been faithful to us. He cannot be otherwise. Let's shift our focus to the memory of His overriding faithfulness, then begin acting on that. How about an "upcast" soul for a change?

Keep yourselves in the love of God,
expecting the mercy of our Lord
Jesus Christ for eternal life.
Jude 21

Every now and then, someone says to me, "Beth, I wish I had an exciting story like yours. Mine has been so boring." Beloved, listen up. If you know Jesus Christ, you have embarked on an amazing adventure. He is never boring.

The only difference between you and me is perhaps that I have been forced to analyze and articulate my journey with Him. When you do the same, you will also wake up to the realization that you have been on a wild ride all along. Maybe you've just been napping through part of it. It's time to wake up and feel the wind in your face!

When Simon Peter saw this, he fell at
Jesus' knees and said, "Go away from me,
because I'm a sinful man, Lord!"
Luke 5:8

If you and I would really start believing
God, we will undoubtedly see His mighty
acts as never before. At times God has
been so palpable that He's nearly scared
me to death.

I've spent most of my life pursuing
God, and if I believe anything at all, I believe that He exists and that He is who
He says He is. But every now and then—
for just a moment—He does something
that removes all doubt, and I find myself
in near physical pain, wanting to cry out,
"Woe is me!" I almost can't handle the
exposure. May we never grow too casual
to forget what we have seen.

Jesus, knowing in Himself that
His disciples were complaining about this,
asked them, "Does this offend you?"
John 6:61

When God appoints us to wait on Him in an important matter, God forbid that we'd return to our whining and complaining that God never does anything for us. If we receive surpassing revelations from Him and don't prove grateful, I don't think we'd be off base to imagine that we could end up in a future bondage exceeding any past bondage we have experienced.

Praise God, He will never break His covenant with us, and He will still hear us every time we cry, but the meantime could be painful. Lest we ever forget, responsibility accompanies revelation.

No one can come to Me unless the
Father who sent Me draws him, and
I will raise him up on the last day.

John 6:44

By believing God was there all along—
wooing us, planning for us, loving us, and
contending with those who contended
with us—we are getting to infuse our
pasts with present-active-participle faith.
Who said we can't change the past?

When we allow God to change the
way we *see* our past, the power of our past
changes dramatically. In a wonderful way,
we get to go back to situations in which
we feel we've been unfaithful to God and
fill them with retroactive faith: belief that
God can do miraculous good even with
terrible failure. We get to step over the
confines of time . . . backwards.

He adds: "I will never again
remember their sins and
their lawless acts."
Hebrews 10:17

How does God's apparent ability to drop
something out of His mind like dirty
clothes through a laundry chute fit into
His omniscience, His infinite ability to
know all things? I believe that if God's
primary way of remembering is to act on
behalf of what He remembers, His primary way of remembering no more is to
no longer act on that memory.

God remembers our sins no more
because the work of the cross already has.
No further sacrifice remains for sin because the work has already been accomplished. Therefore, God need never act
again on their behalf.

Forgive us our sins, for we ourselves also forgive everyone in debt to us. And do not bring us into temptation.

Luke 11:4

Try telling a victim of childhood abuse that forgetting is the heart of forgiving. Try telling a husband or wife whose spouse committed adultery that forgetting is the heart of forgiving. Try telling the mother of a victim of drunk driving that forgetting is the heart of forgiving. They'll never forget.

I'll never forget that I was victimized as a child, but to the glory of my healing God, I can tell you that I never act on it anymore. And because the memories get so little behavioral cooperation anymore, they come to the surface less and less. To me, that's what I call forgetting.

You love Him, though you have
not seen Him. And though not seeing
Him now, you believe in Him.

1 Peter 1:8

Though we have much in common with
Christ's first motley crew of followers, our experiences also vary. You and I
haven't seen the Lord face-to-face as the
first disciples did. Yes, their faith was gi-
gantic, but it was also fueled by sight.

At first glance, you and I and all who
have composed the church of Jesus Christ
through the centuries may seem to be at a
decided advantage. But Christ has promised blessing to those of us who have not
seen with our own eyes and yet believe.
If He honored the tenacious faith of the
disciples who had seen Him in person,
how much more will He honor ours.

He said to them all, "If anyone wants to
come with Me, he must deny himself,
take up his cross daily, and follow Me."
Luke 9:23

Two parts of a compound word leap
from this verse from the Gospel of Luke:
any and *one*. The first part—*any*—speaks
to me about Christ's ready willingness
to lead whoever will follow. We don't
have to be particularly gifted, educated,
or experienced. The second half—*one*—
reminds me that Christ still extends His
invitation to individuals.

In ways our finite minds can hardly
comprehend, Christ died for millions of
ones. Yes, One died for all, but all come
as one. Though His sacrifice was made
for the many, our relationship with Him
is one that is intensely personal.

The one who sows to his flesh will reap
corruption from the flesh, but the one who
sows to the Spirit will reap eternal life.
Galatians 6:8

When we seek God, we will find Him.
And when we find Him, we will ultimately find our callings. When we find
our callings, let's persist in them, not at-
tempting to do a thousand things well
but fanning our gifts into a flame and
pursuing excellence in a few. If we do, we
will reap!

The harvest may not become obvious
in our lifetime, but it will surely come. So
thank Him in advance every time you
sow. Tirelessly plant the things of the
Spirit in the soil of earth. Let nothing
make you quit. Though the harvest tarry,
it will surely come.

My God will supply all
your needs according to His riches
in glory in Christ Jesus.
Philippians 4:19

Many of us have a bad taste in our mouths about the subject of faith and money, because we've seen so many abuses through the media. What a tragedy, however, to let the abuses keep us from practicing believing prayer for the right uses of our finances.

When money is not a god to us and we have a need or godly desire, our heavenly Father welcomes our petitions and our acknowledgment that He is the giver of all good things. May He hear our hearts and heal any skewed thinking we may have about Him and money, inviting us to trust Him for our full supply.

Jesus said, "You of little faith!
Why are you discussing among yourselves
that you do not have bread?"
Matthew 16:8

Anyone can be a mighty warrior in the kingdom of God, and goodness knows we are occupying planet Earth during a time of great spiritual war. But examine any great story of the heroes of church history, and you'll see the same keys that lead to explosively powerful lives: learn how to wield the sword of the Spirit, raise the shield of faith, and pray, pray, pray!

Let's admit our weaknesses, cease our cheap imitations, follow good examples, and position ourselves for the miracles of God. And never forget that the greatest miracle of all occurs each time a human heart is wholly offered to Jesus.

You who occupy the mountain summit,
though you elevate your nest like the eagle,
even from there I will bring you down.
Jeremiah 49:16

When God knew I had gone as far as I
could go without my taking an in-depth
look at my own pitiful flesh, He shattered
my pride and confidence like a sledgehammer through a looking glass.

I would give almost anything to save
someone else the humiliation I endured.
I have no words to express my gratitude
for the work He ultimately accomplished,
but for years I was haunted by the tortur-
ous question, "Couldn't there have been
an easier way?" Finally I accepted the answer: apparently not. My God loves me
too much not to have chosen another
way if it would have sufficed.

All His works are true and
His ways are just. And He is able to
humble those who walk in pride.
Daniel 4:37

God wants to bear much fruit in every one of our lives. He wants to infuse our prayer lives with inconceivable power. He wants to stun us with affirmative answers. He wants to leave the marks of the cross we carry in His name on our Promised Lands and our surrounding spheres of influence.

God longs to do all these things and more in any life who will let Him, but He will not tolerate any of our attempts—however subtle or falsely modest—to share His glory. His Word tells us that we can either humble ourselves or He can humble us.

Humble yourselves therefore
under the mighty hand of God, so that
He may exalt you in due time.

1 Peter 5:6

Unless you physically cannot, I urge you to make a practice of literally getting on the floor, facedown and prostrate before God on a regular basis. Every time you have a smug sense of self-righteousness, buckle your knees before God buckles them for you.

I have often said what some have not wanted to hear—that we, the children of God, can either bend our knees or eventually He will break our legs . . . in one form or another. He is Lord. He is Lord! But He is also a Lord who loves nothing more than to raise up the humble and astonish them with His wonderful works.

SEPTEMBER

The weapons of our warfare are not
fleshly, but are powerful through God for
the demolition of strongholds.

2 Corinthians 10:4

From the moment God first issued the
promise of land to Abram, He described
its occupants as quickly as its perimeters:
"the land of the Kenites, Kenizzites, Kad-
monites, Hittites, Perizzites, Rephaim,
Amorites, Canaanites, Girgashites, and
Jebusites" (Gen. 15:19–21).

One of the reasons why God made
the Israelites fight some tall opposition
for the Promised Land (rather than just
deeding it to them) was so they'd develop
the strength to keep it once they'd conquered it. Surely another was to let them
experience the thrill of victory that only
a hard-fought battle can bring.

Ask about the ancient paths:
Which is the way to what is good?
Then take it and find rest for yourselves.
Jeremiah 6:16

Like the Israelites, you and I have been promised spiritual ground for great and abiding victory on a turf where our enemy stands in defiance. If you're not presently occupying your Promised Land, rest assured the devil is. Are you going to stand by and let him get away with that?

God has given you land, Beloved, but He's calling you to go forth and take it. Your enemy is standing on your God-given ground, just daring you to take possession of it. Are you going to let him have it? Or are you going to claim your inheritance? Possession is the law of the Promised Land. Red Rover, go over.

The LORD commanded me to teach you
statutes and ordinances for you to follow in
the land you are about to cross into.

Deuteronomy 4:14

The Creator of heaven and earth—the
One who has the entire universe and its
riches at His very disposal—knows you
by name, has planned a Promised Land
for you, and longs to bless you. But He
wisely reserves the right to require your
cooperation.

Many promises of God are unconditional, but His promises of full-throttle
blessing, abiding, fruit-bearing, and conquering are not. Promised Land theology
becomes an earthbound reality only to
those who cash in their fear and complacency for the one ticket out of their long-
inhabited wilderness.

The life I now live in the flesh,
I live by faith in the Son of God, who
loved me and gave Himself for me.
Galatians 2:20

Whether or not we like the concept, Christ loves to respond to us according to our faith. I used to bristle over this idea until I started exercising a little more belief and experienced completely unexpected and exceeding results.

In fact, I've noted a pretty reliable ratio along the way: the less faith we have, the more we tend to resent the concept. Maybe you're bristling about it right now. But let me just go ahead and say what this certified sanguine is thinking: nothing on earth is more fun than faith. If you decide to sign up for the great adventure of faith, I can promise you'll never get bored.

He demonstrated this power in the Messiah
by raising Him from the dead and seating
Him at His right hand in the heavens.
Ephesians 1:20

God exerts an incomparable power in
the lives of those who continue believing
Him. Nothing on earth compares to the
strength God is willing to interject into
lives caught in the act of believing.

Can you think of any need you might
have that would require more strength
than God exerted when He raised His
Son from the dead? Me neither. He can
raise marriages from the dead and re-
store life and purpose to those who have
given up. He can forgive and purify the
vilest sinner. God's specialty is raising
dead things to life and making impossible things possible.

I am saying this for your
own benefit . . . so that you may be
devoted to the Lord without distraction.

1 Corinthians 7:35

Anytime someone makes fun of me or tells me I'm too radical or demonstrative for them, I always have the same thought: "Beloved, I was once the most bound-up, defeated believer you've ever met, and now I'm a walking miracle experiencing the power of God. With all due respect, how's life going for you?"

Sometimes God demands radical measures when He wants to bring about radical results. I may look silly, but to the glory of God, something's working. This woman should have been a lost cause. I just hope God takes each of us to a place we've never been with Him before.

The one who loves Me will be
loved by My Father. I also will love him
and will reveal Myself to him.
John 14:21

I believe that a significant measure of
spiritual vision is developed simply by
watching. The more we "see" God at
work, the more we'll believe. And the
more we believe, the more we're liable to
see.

As you participate with God in the
increase of your faith and sanctification,
God will undoubtedly be at significant
work in your life. He accomplishes so
much, we don't have eyes to see it all. But
if He's willing to make some of His work
and a measure of His presence observ-
able, I want to stop all distractions for a
moment and see it. Don't you?

When Jesus heard it,
He answered him, "Don't be afraid.
Only believe, and she will be made well."
Luke 8:50

We must cease to accept the visible as if it's the only possible solution and start believing what God says over what man sees. Could any restlessness and dissatisfaction we feel in our souls be Christ initiating and authorizing a new day of awakened faith and outpoured Spirit? Oh, God, let it be!

Please don't misunderstand me to say that believing God only involves believing Him for dramatic miracles in our lives and in the lives of others. But if we don't include believing Him for the miraculous, can you imagine the tragedy of all we could miss?

If the ministry of condemnation
had glory, the ministry of righteousness
overflows with even more glory.
2 Corinthians 3:9

At the Last Supper, Christ introduced
a term with revolutionary implications.
As He raised the cup, He said, "This cup
is the new covenant established by My
blood; it is shed for you" (Luke 22:20).

You and I are under the new covenant. And if we understood the fullness
of the implications, we'd shout, "Glory!"
Indeed, that would be the key word. We
look upon the lives of people like Moses
and wish we had such manifestations and
revelations of divine presence. But if we
really understood the meaning of the
verse above, we'd not only shout, "Glory!"
We'd shout, "Surpassing glory!"

When you judge another,
you condemn yourself, since you,
the judge, do the same things.

Romans 2:1

If we want to be filled with faith and behold some wonders, we are wise to avoid giving in to two temptations: judging and arguing.

Whatever we do, we must avoid judging someone else for a weaker or lesser faith. I have enough fear of God in me to know that I will likely be tested on the very things I've judged in others.

But don't argue with them either. Nothing is logical about miracles. Therefore, to the degree that we debate matters of faith, we could find ourselves drained of it. Keep seeking. Keep believing. And count on God to take care of the rest.

Look at how great a love the Father
has given us, that we should be called
God's children. And we are!

1 John 3:1

Who does God say we are? He spent no
small amount of ink expressing the various facets of sonship (and daughtership).
For example:

"He chose us in Him, before the
foundation of the world, to be holy and
blameless in His sight. In love He predestined us to be adopted through Jesus
Christ for Himself, according to His favor and will, to the praise of His glorious
grace that He favored us with in the Beloved" (Eph. 1:4–6).

If we knew nothing else but these
few truths and accepted them into our
belief system, our lives would be altered.

God's righteousness is revealed
from faith to faith, just as it is written:
"The righteous will live by faith."
Romans 1:17

If the thought of God's accepting us by faith alone causes the mercury in our self-righteousness meters to rise, we may still be trying to take some credit for our acceptable standing before God through Christ. Grace is humbling, isn't it?

Reminds me of the time my daughter Amanda called me on her cell phone to tell me she had just driven beside a car with a bumper sticker that read, "What if the hokeypokey is what it's all about?" After a good laugh, the thought came to me that on the biblical subject of righteousness, faith *is* what it's all about. Stick that in your song and dance to it.

My life is down in the dust;
give me life through Your word. I told You
about my life, and You listened to me.
Psalm 119:25–26

For years I lived in a cycle of poor self-image followed by poor choices feeding a poorer self-image and even poorer choices. I was a Christian, so this was not due to my being in an unredeemed or ignorant state. It was directly due to believing my past's prediction over my future rather than God's Word.

When I began to study the Scripture in-depth, I had no idea that God's first purpose for stirring in me an insatiable appetite for His Word was to perform intense surgery on my broken heart and distorted mind. But that's what happens when we believe who God says we are.

Teach me Your way, LORD,
and I will live by Your truth. Give me an
undivided mind to fear Your name.
Psalm 86:11

Through a study of the Word in my latter twenties, I came upon Scripture after Scripture characterizing a child of God. Soon I began to believe them for others. But I was unwilling and hesitant to apply these same Scriptures to myself.

Surely someone besides me has confidently assured a hurting or questioning person of a biblical truth that applied to him or her as a child of God, though you wouldn't accept it for yourself. Perhaps you've also noticed that God doesn't put up with that for very long. He is adamant that we allow Him to teach *to* us what He wants to teach *through* us.

Do not be afraid or discouraged
because of this vast multitude, for the
battle is not yours, but God's.
2 Chronicles 20:15

The common word "discouraged" means
all the things you might imagine, but I
found there is one English synonym that
is worthy of particular meditation and
thought: "demoralization."

As I reflected on the ramifications
of this word—demoralization—I felt like
the Holy Spirit revealed an insight to me
concerning one possible dimension of it.
I believe demoralization can occur when
Satan figures out who you and I fear most
that we are—and what we fear most that
we cannot do—then he sets out to con-
firm it. When you see that happening,
you can know he's at work. Again.

"It's a ghost!" they said, and cried out
in fear. Immediately Jesus spoke to them.
"Have courage! It is I. Don't be afraid."
Matthew 14:26–27

When God told Joshua not to be terrified or discouraged upon entering the Promised Land, He gave him the important reason. It had nothing to do with the absence of terrifying or discouraging circumstances. On the contrary, Joshua had never faced anything so frightful or potentially disparaging in his life.

What reason did God give Joshua for turning from fear and discouragement in the face of huge opposition? The same reason Jesus gave to His disciples not to be afraid in the storm. It wasn't the removal of their frightful circumstances but the presence of their Savior.

I know the plans I have for you . . .
plans for your welfare, not for disaster,
to give you a future and a hope.

Jeremiah 29:11

I honestly thought my genuine love for God would keep my handicapped feet on the path all by itself. I clearly remember telling God in my twenties that no one would ever love Him more than I and that He'd never be sorry He called me.

Then I fell headfirst into a pit—not for the first time or, tragically, the last. Over and over the words rung in my head like church bells drowning in discord: I failed God! I failed God! Somehow I don't think I'm the only one who ever felt that way. But He knows the plans He has for you. Plans to give you a hope and a future. You can because *He* can.

If I say: "I won't mention Him or
speak any longer in His name," His message
becomes a fire burning in my heart.
Jeremiah 20:9

When we are filled with the Holy Spirit
by yielding to His lordship, and we read
and receive God's Word, something virtually supernatural takes place.

Picture the Holy Spirit like a flam-
mable substance within us. (Because oil
was often associated with anointing in
the Bible, many scholars believe oil sym-
bolized the Holy Spirit.) Next, imagine
taking the torch of God's Word and com-
bining it with the oil of the Holy Spirit.
What is the result? The consuming fire
of God blazes within us, bringing supernatural energy, glorious activity, and pure,
unadulterated power.

I tell you, all the things you pray
and ask for—believe that you have
received them, and you will have them.
Mark 11:24

News flash: we should be experiencing lots of answered prayer. Lots of it. But I have a feeling much of the body of Christ feels like I did for so long. I prayed all the usual "bless and protect us" prayers, but my ordinary mode of operation was to pray things that looked like they were probably going to turn out anyway.

I doubt many believers ever grow to the point that they know the mind of Christ well enough to continually pray petitions He answers affirmatively. We can, however, mature in our prayer life to the point that we see far more affirmative answers than we previously have.

Even though He had performed
so many signs in their presence,
they did not believe in Him.
John 12:37

I got a sense one day that, frankly, God was bored with my prayer life. He seemed to be saying, "My child, you believe me for so little. Don't be so safe in the things you pray. Who are you trying to keep from looking foolish? Me or you?"

See, sometimes I decided I'd rather not ask for certain things than risk a no. I reasoned that God was sovereign and I'd simply let Him do what He wanted. In reality, I was terrified that God or I would let me down and shake what little faith I had. The question I heard from the Holy Spirit still convicts and chills me. Is He asking you something similar?

Through the proof of this service,
they will glorify God for your obedience to
the confession of the gospel of Christ.
2 Corinthians 9:13

We could think of many examples where obedience comes from faith. Sometimes, for instance, we have to exercise faith to believe that obedience to God in a difficult situation will ultimately bear fruit, even though it looks as though it might immediately cause hardship.

We also have to exercise faith to believe God can handle the consequences of our obedience if someone important to us is not going to approve first.

For many of us, the step of faith begins much further back: we have to exercise faith to believe we are even capable of long-term obedience. And we are.

As you have received Christ Jesus the Lord,
walk in Him, rooted and built up in Him
and established in the faith.
Colossians 2:6–7

I often speak and apply Scripture when I
vocalize my most serious prayer requests.
I also might use Scripture over matters
that require long periods of time, such as
the salvation of a resistant sibling. I often
interject Scripture into requests for miraculous intervention, as well.

Each of these represents a time when
we're most tempted to dwindle in faith,
energy, and longevity in prayer. But by
using Scripture, I transfer the burden
to God's Word rather than my ability to
pray correctly or adequately. Because it is
from God's divine mouth, His Word has
energy all its own. I let it do the work.

Now He has reconciled you by His physical
body through His death, to present you holy,
faultless, and blameless before Him.

Colossians 1:22

One way God hammered a biblical identity into my belief system was through
a number of *this and that* conversations.
When I saw Scriptures characterizing a
child of God, I constantly sensed Him
saying to my heart, "Beth, you are *this*."
For a long time, I responded, "No, Lord,
I am *that*"—one of the hurtful things I
thought about myself.

Months turned into years, and the
voice of God grew increasingly insistent:
"Beth, when will you ever believe you
are *this*?" He was getting me to the point
where, even though I may have felt like a
that, he wanted me thinking like a *this*.

We are the circumcision, the ones who serve
by the Spirit of God, boast in Christ Jesus,
and do not put confidence in the flesh.
Philippians 3:3

With a mustard seed of faith to at least
believe I was *this* even though I felt like a
that, God brought about a breakthrough.
With constant doses of His Word and
a growing cooperation in my heart, He
taught me to believe Him enough to at
least start making decisions like a *this.*

I would come to a crossroad of decision and think, "I still feel like *that,* but
God says I'm *this.* How would a *this* behave in my current situation?" I'd picture
someone who I knew was a *this* and try to
imagine what she'd do. And over time my
habits began to change. I started behav-
ing like a *this.* After all, *this* is who I am.

We have received grace . . . through Him to
bring about the obedience of faith among all
the nations, on behalf of His name.

Romans 1:5

All the while I was preoccupied with *this*
and *that,* Romans 1:5 was hard at work. My
obedience flowed directly from my faith
to believe I was who God said I was, even
when I didn't feel like it. Not surprising-
ly, the more I acted like *this* instead of *that*,
the more I felt blessed, chosen, adopted,
favored, redeemed, and forgiven.

I guess that's why I'm like a dog
gnawing on a bone in my unceasing insistence that anyone can live victoriously.
Anyone can know the fruit of obedience.
Dear (equally hardheaded?) one, if I can
live victoriously through the power of the
Holy Spirit, anyone can.

Simon, Simon, look out! Satan has asked
to sift you like wheat. But I have prayed
for you that your faith may not fail.
Luke 22:31–32

Why did Jesus pray specifically for Simon
Peter's faith not to fail? Because Peter's
future was not dependent on a perfect
track record. It was dependent upon his
faith. Peter would desperately need the
courage to believe he was still who Christ
said he was even after such failure. He
would need to believe God knowing that
it was credited to him as righteousness.

For some reason, the hardest biblical truths to accept are the ones about us.
But don't let that be said of you. Believe
you are who God says you are, and fath-
om the double blessing of God crediting
it to you as righteousness.

If you have faith the size of a mustard seed,
you will tell this mountain, "Move from
here to there," and it will move.
Matthew 17:20

Do you remember when Christ spoke
these words to His disciples? The next
words out of his mouth were these:
"Nothing will be impossible for you."
Christ did not tell his disciples only to
"think" with faith-filled authority, nor
did He tell them to perform certain
physical demonstrations. He distinctive-
ly told them to have faith and to "tell this
mountain" what it needed to do.

In other words, I think we could say
Christ taught His disciples to "believe
and therefore speak." I think we, too,
could speak to some mountains at appropriate times, and they just might move.

When they hear, immediately
Satan comes and takes away the
word sown in them.

Mark 4:15

In case the thought of telling mountains
to move makes you nervous, let me assure
you that I, too, have seen the misuse and
abuse of concepts like this through practices that involve disturbing shouts and
rebukes (as if the louder the better) and
presumptuous naming and claiming. My
plea is that we not miss the use because
of misuse.

The concept of God assigning or
entrusting limited authority to His children under the umbrella of His own is
consistent from Genesis to Revelation.
Satan has much to gain by turning us off
to faith practices.

If you believe,
you will receive whatever
you ask for in prayer.
Matthew 21:22

If we truly believe according to the sound application of Scripture that God is extending authority to us as His children over a certain matter, we might be shocked what we could tell to "Move!" and it would. I've tried telling a few mountains to move at times (mostly in private) and, lo and behold, to this Baptist girl's surprise, some have!

I've had some fun learning to exercise my weak and awkward faith—and even to see it grow a bit—on "mountains" that have taken any number of forms. I don't mind telling you that I think God has gotten a kick out of it, too.

These are opposed to each other, so that you
don't do what you want. But if you are led by
the Spirit, you are not under the law.

Galatians 5:17–18

Any supernatural results that arise from
biblical practices come from God alone.
If a mountain moves, God moved it. He
simply invited us to join Him by allowing us to exhale a powerful breath of the
Spirit.

Having the faith to tell a mountain
to move and asking God to move the
mountain are not opposing concepts.
Like many biblical practices, we don't replace one with the other. We seek to be
led by the Holy Spirit and discern when
to implement certain practices. God
alone must be the one and only initiator
in matters of faith.

OCTOBER

A joyful heart makes
a face cheerful, but a sad heart
produces a broken spirit.

Proverbs 15:13

Would you be offended if I told you that I not only think God is awesome, wonderful, and faithful but that I also think He is fun? In fact, in my opinion those who take the faith out of spiritual living have taken the fun out of life. They can play it safe if they want, but I like living out on a limb with God.

I've put all my hopes and all my faith in Him. I have absolutely nothing else to hang on to. I'm banking on God and His Word with every drop of energy I have. If He doesn't come through, I've made a fool of myself. But I'm not worried about it, because He has yet to fail me.

Lies and not faithfulness prevail in the land,
for they proceed from one evil to another,
and they do not take Me into account.
Jeremiah 9:3

Your tongue—just like mine—has most likely been misused and misappropriated countless times. As if our own tendencies aren't bad enough, we also live among a people of unclean lips. Many of us live or work in environments where backbiting, gossip, lying, profanity, and off-color remarks and jokes are pandemic.

God wants to send you and me forth into our worlds in His name. And the instrument of His greatest potential use in each of our lives is the tongue. No, we're not all called to speak, teach, or preach, but we are all called to use our mouths to glorify His name.

We should wash ourselves clean from every
impurity of the flesh and spirit, making our
sanctification complete in the fear of God.
2 Corinthians 7:1

Jesus Christ graced earth's guilty sod to
offer Himself as the perfect sacrifice and
fulfill every requirement of the Law. He
shed His blood on an altar constructed
of two pieces of wood and fashioned into
a cross. Because the fire of holy judgment
met with the blood of the spotless Lamb,
we need no other act of atonement.

But we are desperate for the continuing work of sanctification. Too much
power is at stake to continue cultivat-
ing an inconsistent and unconsecrated
mouth. The challenge of a tamed tongue
is so great that we'd be wise to give it daily
attention in prayer.

In the year that King Uzziah died,
I saw the Lord seated on a high and lofty
throne, and His robe filled the temple.

Isaiah 6:1

Today you and I stand before the same throne the prophet Isaiah approached in his glorious vision. God is just as holy, Just as high and lifted up. The train of His robe still fills the temple, and the seraphs still cry, "Holy!"

But the writer of Hebrews 4:15–16 tells us that because we have Jesus as our great High Priest, we boldly approach a throne of *grace*. And the same grace that saves also sanctifies. We need not hang our heads and beg. All we need do is lift up our faces and ask. May Jesus touch our lips again with coals from the altar and set our tongues aflame with holy fire.

But on the seventh day, march around the
city seven times. . . . Then the city wall will
collapse, and the people will advance.
Joshua 6:4–5

When the Israelites marched around
Jericho, their seventh trip around on the
seventh day could not have seemed any
different from the rest, with the exception that they felt wearier. Why did God
purpose for the wall to fall on that particular round? Because it was time.

Day-in and day-out, the fundamentals are the way I march repeatedly
around my Jerichos. Unlike Joshua and
the children of Israel, I never know when
my present Jericho is going to fall. I just
know that I'm to keep believing and keep
marching. When the time is complete,
the wall is going to collapse.

My foes will rejoice because I am shaken.
But I have trusted in Your faithful love;
my heart will rejoice in Your deliverance.
Psalm 13:4–5

You and I have each experienced times when we've prayed our hardest for two different people to be healed of physical illness. One is delivered on earth; the other is delivered in heaven.

We've also prayed for people struggling to make ends meet. One gets a job; sometimes the other loses her home.

So why does God so often bring such different results from the same depth of earnest, believing prayer? 1) We don't know; 2) we're not supposed to know; and 3) we're not responsible for the One who does. We are not God. We are His children.

Often a spirit seizes him . . . and it throws him into convulsions. . . . I begged Your disciples to drive it out, but they couldn't.

Luke 9:39–40

As we deeply desire to love and help people, we must be careful not to allow them to make us feel responsible for getting something from God or explaining His mysterious actions. If we do, we are letting them make us false christs, and we have escorted them not only into inevitable disappointment but into idolatry.

Jesus' first followers were surely in these kinds of positions constantly. They lived and loved by faith but, remember, they didn't get everything they asked for either. God must reason that the hearts and minds of mortals can't handle unwavering success, even in spiritual terms.

What then can we say
that Abraham, our forefather
according to the flesh, has found?
Romans 4:1

Abraham and David lived in different eras and fulfilled different positions, yet they shared one commonality that related heavily to the concept of faith being credited as righteousness. Both had sinned so grievously that faith was demanded for them to believe they were still who God said they were: a father of multitudes and a king whose kingdom would never end. True restoration demands faith.

God can credit our faith as righteousness without concern that we'll take advantage of the freedom. He knows faith that doesn't lead to obedience is all talk and no walk.

You are My witnesses . . . so that
you may know and believe Me and
understand that I am He.
Isaiah 43:10

Believing God doesn't happen on special occasions or sudden demand. Present-active-participle believing is a lifestyle— a daily, deliberate choice. It is a belief that awakens God in the morning and says, "Lord, I thank You for another day to know You and believe You. Whatever means You may choose to increase my faith today, I commit myself to that glorious end."

After He sings us to sleep at night, may our Father be able to look at the Son on His right and say, "She believed Me today." He will credit it to our account as righteousness.

We are convinced that we have a
clear conscience, wanting to conduct
ourselves honorably in everything.
Hebrews 13:18

All—such a small word means so much.
But never in history has the concept of
giving everything to one chief end been
so challenged. We have never been more
fragmented or have lived in a society that
demanded more pieces of us. How can a
person who is giving a thousand pieces of
herself to innumerable demands and desires ever know wholeness?

The Lord Jesus offers us the one and
only way to wholeness: giving ourselves
wholly to Him. Every fish. Every loaf.
Withholding nothing. We give Christ
our all. And with it He is able to do the
impossible.

The anointing you received
from Him remains in you. . . . His
anointing teaches you about all things.

1 John 2:27

I ache for the body of Christ in our generation to learn how to tarry before God and expectantly wait for Him to speak. I'm desperate to learn it for myself. If we do, what revelation we would receive! We cannot have a drive-thru relationship with God and expect to behold His glory.

Like the children of Israel, much of the body of Christ still stands back and watches those they consider truly anointed draw near to God's glory. Dear One, *you* are anointed! Never settle for a secondhand relationship. Never be satisfied with distant glory.

I will give them a heart to know Me,
that I am the LORD. They will be My
people, and I will be their God.

Jeremiah 24:7

Great faith is born nowhere else but in
the presence of God. There is only one
way we can know that God is who He
says He is, and that is by knowing God.

The more we know God, the more
we will believe Him. And the more we
choose to believe Him, the more we will
get to know Him.

This is the cycle that replaces "believe
little, see little; believe less, see less." The
know-believe cycle is the one we want to
be pedaling for the rest of our days! The
way that we birth faith is by knowing the
One we believe, then we walk our faith
by believing the One we know.

I know whom I have believed and am
persuaded that He is able to guard what has
been entrusted to me until that day.

2 Timothy 1:12

The God to whom you commit yourself and everything that concerns you is huge. He is the omnipotent Maker of heaven and earth. He is the One who sees. He is the One who knows. He is the One who acts on behalf of His children.

He is the Mighty Warrior. He is the compassionate Father. He is the Way, the Truth, and the Life. He is the coming King.

He is love. He is light. He is good. He is right. He is your soul's delight. He is whatever you need. He alone is wise. In Him alone life makes sense, and apart from Him all is chaos.

I know your works; you
have a reputation for being
alive, but you are dead.
Revelation 3:1

If God were to give the worldwide church of Jesus Christ a grade today, as He did to the seven churches in Revelation, I fear we'd receive an "F" for faith. Most of us—and certainly I—have been tightly chained, smugly satisfied, and dangerously arrogant through unbelief.

But I am convinced that God is calling the body of Christ to a vast revival of a very specific nature: a revival of biblical faith. I see a fresh emphasis springing up all over. This faith realization is birthed through an eye-opening realization and authentic repentance of the far-reaching plague of unbelief.

Do you believe only because
I told you I saw you under the fig tree?
You will see greater things than this.
John 1:50

Over the past years, God has challenged me and empowered me to change. And never in my history with God have I received more blatant approval from Him over a newly directed approach. I still research the Word with the same fervor and pursue sound scholarship, but now I intentionally add my faith to it.

In other words, I actively say, "God infuse these words not only into my heart and mind but also into the marrow of my belief system. Bring these words to life in me today. Help me not only to learn them but also to walk by faith in them. Help me believe You."

We have come to know and to believe the
love that God has for us. God is love, and the
one who remains in love remains in God.

1 John 4:16

Today, even when I miss the mark in
making sound application of a biblical
truth or when I misread a spiritual signal
from the Lord, I've sensed Him saying
to my heart, "You're on the right track,
child. Stay after it! Keep practicing belief,
and you'll learn more and more about
My desires as you go."

One of my new mottoes has become,
"If I err, let me err on the side of belief."
Scripture makes me confident that God
looks on the heart. I'd much rather Him
see misguided actions from my believing
heart than safe-and-sound actions from
an unbelieving heart.

Now faith is the reality
of what is hoped for, the proof
of what is not seen.
Hebrews 11:1

The words "hoped for" and "not seen" in the verse above should quickly suggest that we aren't likely to make an exact science of faith. The nature of walking by faith rather than by sight comes with its obvious risks.

One of the inevitable questions each person challenged to believe God has to answer is whether she is willing to risk being wrong from time to time. Faith may not be palatable to perfectionists for this very reason. Thankfully, I gave up on perfection a long time ago. I've found that a continual commitment to the pursuit of balance steers me back on course.

The law perfected nothing,
but a better hope is introduced, through
which we draw near to God.
Hebrews 7:19

One positive result of past failure is that you surrender the pursuit of perfection and, if you've gained any sense along the way, you replace it with the pursuit of God's redemption.

Nothing is more redemptive than faith in God. You learn that failure may be painful, but it's rarely fatal.

After coming to grips with the high premium God places on our faith, I refuse to give up a life practice of believing God just because I accidentally swerve off the road a few times in my faith journey. Hebrews 11:6 says *faith* is what pleases God, not perfection.

Grant that Your slaves may speak Your
message with complete boldness, while You
stretch out Your hand for healing.
Acts 4:29–30

I believe God is about to perform a fresh
work in His body of believers, one that
has been calendared in heaven since time
began. And, yes, one that will involve
signs and wonders as He extends His
final saving and judging revelations to
planet Earth.

You and I may not see the kinds of
characterizing signs and wonders His
Word predicts, but we are to prepare for
them by adjusting our faith to the swelling work God is planning to perform.
We must leave the generations that come
behind us a heritage of faith and an invitation to go further still.

It is God who is working in you,
enabling you both to will and
to act for His good purpose.
Philippians 2:13

Does God need our faith before He can act, since He already has the events of the last days planned? Of course not. His purpose from the moment He created humanity was to invite man to partner with Him in His work.

Simply put, faith partners with God. Faith also invites God. Swelling faith can hasten swelling works of God because, frankly, He favors the invitation.

With all my heart, I believe God wants us to ask Him to reveal Himself more blatantly on earth so that many will be saved, others delivered, others helped, and still others healed.

Be imitators of God, as dearly loved
children. And walk in love, as the Messiah
also loved us and gave Himself for us.
Ephesians 5:1–2

Every time I read Ephesians 5:1, I picture
God sending us out the door of our secret place with Him and into the world,
saying, "Now go out there and act like
the dearly loved child you are today. And
not just *anyone's* dearly loved child. Keep
in mind today that your Father created
this world you live in and told the sun to
come up again this morning.

"I'll be sitting here on My throne all
day long. Keep checking in with Me and
let Me know what you need. You have My
cell number: Jeremiah 33:3—'Call to Me
and I will answer you and tell you great
and wondrous things you do not know.'"

Be on your guard, so that your
minds are not dulled . . . or that day
will come on you unexpectedly .

Luke 21:34

The mind is often the last inner chamber
we allow God to sanctify. One reason is
because it is a never-ending challenge to
keep clean, and we sometimes adopt the
attitude, "Why bother?" But, oh, we must
bother because the mind is the biggest
battlefield on which our spiritual battles
are fought. Even our feelings eventually
bow down to our thoughts.

People say, "I can't change the way I
feel." But if we change the way we think—
the way we believe—we will change the
way we feel. It is a demonic doctrine that
says our love for God doesn't feel or that
our minds cannot be clean.

May the God of peace Himself sanctify you completely. And may your spirit, soul, and body be kept sound and blameless.

1 Thessalonians 5:23

A big part of living the sincere, sanctified, believing life is learning how to behave consistently whether we're in the world or in the church.

Something is wrong, for example, if our coworkers would be shocked that we go to church. Most believers don't work in environments where preaching to co-workers is part of their job description, but would coworkers find our behavior inconsistent with the belief system we profess at church?

Relief arises from consistency—from being the same person at the shopping mall as we are at Sunday worship.

Let us hold on to the confession
of our hope without wavering, for
He who promised is faithful.

Hebrews 10:23

God is more than willing to cleanse us
from the guilt of repented sin! He will
never turn us down as we approach Him
on the basis of Christ's accomplished
work on Calvary.

But for us to apply this accomplished
work, we've got to approach Him with a
full assurance of faith. In other words,
we've got to believe God will do what He
says He will do!

Christ has already done the work,
but we must receive it by faith. He wants
nothing more than to give you and me
the grace gift of a fresh, clean conscience,
but we've got to accept it through belief!

After three days, they found Him in the
temple complex sitting among the teachers,
listening to them and asking them questions.

Luke 2:46

In this rare scene of the child Jesus, I am
thankful to see that He not only speaks
but He also listens. And not only does
He listen, He also asks questions.

Contrary to popular opinion, faith
is not the avoidance of questions. In fact,
our faith grows when we seek answers,
and thankfully we find many of them between Genesis 1 and Revelation 22. We
may hear a gentle "Because I said so" to
questions He chooses not to answer, but
I don't believe our heavenly Father is offended by questions. Rather, He is a God
who listens, who allows us to pour out
our hearts to Him.

Martha was distracted by her many tasks, and
she came up and asked, "Lord, don't You care
that my sister has left me to serve alone?"

Luke 10:40

Sometimes we are so shocked when a
seasoned servant of God confesses that
he or she is struggling with belief and an
awareness of God's loving care. We find
ourselves thinking, "You of all people!
You are such a wonderful servant of God.
How can you doubt for a moment how
much He cares for you?"

Could it be that service itself has
somehow distracted this person from
abundant, life-giving intimacy with God?
Christ's love for us never changes. But we
must not neglect to give Him ample time
and opportunity to lavish us with the love
He always feels for us.

Consider the ravens: they don't sow
or reap; they don't have a storeroom
or a barn; yet God feeds them.

Luke 12:24

One of the best ways to become more acquainted with the heart of God is to search the Scriptures and study the things He values most. That's what this verse is all about.

No matter how much value everything else in the world represents to Him, you are more valuable to God than all the rest put together.

As people who act out what we believe through our lifestyles and decisions, we need to take this statement of biblical fact to heart. If we truly believe what God says about our value to Him, our lives will be dramatically altered.

Now to Him who is able to protect
you from stumbling and to make you stand
in the presence of His glory . . .
Jude 24

Even after all our frailties and failures,
Christ Jesus can hardly wait to acknowl-
edge us before the very angels of God. If
He is that unashamed of us in all our im-
perfections, how can we be ashamed of
Him, our Redeemer and Deliverer?

So don't duck your head in shame
under the coffee table. At one time or another, all of us have faced the temptation
to shrink away from openly acknowl-
edging Christ. But I've learned one of
the best ways to get over our attacks of
shame: do it over and over until it loses
its intimidation. The more we practice,
the easier it gets!

Can any of you add a cubit to his height by
worrying? If then you're not able to do even
a little thing, why worry about the rest?

Luke 12:25–26

Why do you think worry is so difficult
to control? Maybe one reason is because
we have so many prime opportunities to
practice it! We're never going to overcome worry by eliminating reasons to
worry. Life isn't suddenly going to fix itself. God wills that we overcome worry
even when overwhelmed by legitimate
reasons to worry.

All our worrying—even when done
in the name of love—can accomplish absolutely nothing. But all our praying in
the name of Jesus could entreat God to
accomplish anything. When will we learn
to turn our worry effort into prayer?

Why are you amazed at this? Or why do you
stare at us, as though by our own power or
godliness we had made him walk?

Acts 3:12

As we actively love others and risk praying big prayers for them, let's not dream
of taking credit when we receive what
we ask. Not only will we offend God and
mislead people, we will place ourselves in
position to take the blame when we *don't*
get what we ask.

I am often reminded of a bumper
sticker I once saw, which succinctly said:
"There is a God. You are not Him." As
the words of Peter attest, none of us possesses enough "power or godliness" to
enact a miracle in someone else's life—
even on our best day. Faith expressing
itself through love is a miracle in itself.

While we are at home in the body
we are away from the Lord—for we
walk by faith, not by sight.
2 Corinthians 5:6–7

You and I have talked a lot about our Promised Lands from the beginning of this book. We started this yearlong journey at the Jordan River's edge, looking into the distance to our Canaan, the land where we've been called to walk by faith and fulfill our divine destinies.

Our land of promise is the place where we abide, actively and presently believing God. It is a good land. A land of harvest and plenty. I pray that you have been moving step-by-step across the dry riverbed, with the waters of the Jordan heaped to each side. Now is no time to quit walking by faith.

NOVEMBER

"Why are you troubled?" He asked them.
"And why do doubts arise in your hearts?
Look at My hands and My feet."
Luke 24:38–39

Christ's willingness to continue drawing us to belief totally astounds me. At no time after appearing to His disciples in resurrected form did He say, "You bunch of idiots! I'm sick of trying to talk you into believing Me!" When the sight of Him wasn't enough, Jesus said, "Look at My hands and My feet."

We ourselves have often seen His hands by way of His constant provision and glorious intervention. We have seen His feet as He's gone before us. Surely we, too, have beheld the hands and feet of Christ with the eyes of faith. May we look again today—and believe!

My dear brothers, be steadfast, immovable,
always excelling in the Lord's work, knowing
that your labor in the Lord is not in vain.

1 Corinthians 15:58

Like me, I'm sure you've been through
seasons when one crisis seems to roll in
behind another, when you're faced with
losses beyond what your heart can bear.
I'm not glad when these troubles happen.
I don't rejoice over loss. But even when
my heart is very sore, I'm aware it's still
beating. I am alive, and life is strangely
abundant.

Had God not taught me His Word
and made Himself the uncontested love
of my life, I think I might have wanted to
quit. If you, too, tend to fear having your
heart broken, ask Him to redirect your
energies toward faithfulness instead.

You were called to this, because Christ also
suffered for you, leaving you an example,
so that you should follow in His steps.

1 Peter 2:21

Hardship sometimes comes as a direct
result of sin and disobedience. We are
usually aware when consequences of sin
have caused us deep suffering, but many
other times, trials have nothing to do
with disobedience. Yet we may wonder
why we can't muster enough faith to be
healthy, problem-free, and prosperous.

Please be encouraged to know that
difficulty is not a sign of immaturity or
faithlessness. The Holy Spirit will do His
job and let you know if you're suffering
because of sin. Otherwise, remember—
we all suffer many hardships. The key
difference is this: ours are never in vain.

This man Paul has persuaded and misled
a considerable number of people by saying
that gods made by hand are not gods!

Acts 19:26

The Ephesians believed that the image of the goddess Artemis had fallen from heaven. Some scholars assume they were describing a meteor that hit Ephesus, which the people imagined to look like a multi-breasted woman. I am sometimes amazed at the things people believe.

I'm no rocket scientist, but I find Paul's message of a Messiah sent from God who offers eternal life to everyone who believes much more plausible than that. Yes, God requires faith, but not as much as a number of belief systems falling out of the skies today. Go ahead and believe Him. He's very believable.

Speaking the truth in love,
let us grow in every way into Him
who is the head—Christ.
Ephesians 4:15

The best way for a child of God to avoid
being kidnapped is to stay close to home.
Children in natural families cannot live
their entire lives in their yards, but children in the spiritual family of God can!
Continuing to live in Christ means remaining close to Him, retaining a focus
on Him. Any other focus can easily lead
to deception.

Many of us have probably let something become a bigger focus than Christ
Himself, even if that focus was on a biblical teaching or doctrine. But we are far
less likely to be kidnapped when we stay
focused on the Head, Jesus Christ.

[God] keeps His gracious covenant loyalty
for a thousand generations with those who
love Him and keep His commands.

Deuteronomy 7:9

I once thought Exodus 20:5, which refers
to the sins of the fathers being visited
upon the children, was one of the scari-
est verses in the Bible. Then I found that
the word "visit" means to take a census
or head count. In other words, when a
parent practices sin and rebellion, God
can take a census in that family and find
those continuing results.

But sin and rebellion are not the only
heritage passed down to future generations. Let your children see the sincerity
of your faith. Let them see you praying
and trusting. Nothing carries the weight
of sincere faith!

We always pray for you that our
God will . . . fulfill every desire for
goodness and the work of faith.
2 Thessalonians 1:11

God can deliver anyone from anything at
any time. He doesn't need any help. Yet
He invites us to be part of His great work
through prayer.

Never underestimate the effects of
intercessory prayer lifted for our deliverance. Never underestimate the effect of
prayer for others. If we don't intercede
for one another, we miss opportunities
to see His deliverance and to thank Him
for His faithfulness.

I call this God's profit-sharing plan.
When we pray for one another, we share
the blessings when His deliverance comes
because we've been personally involved.

Don't be afraid, Paul. You must stand before
Caesar. And, look! God has graciously given
you all those who are sailing with you.

Acts 27:24

The effects of one person's actions can be
like an umbrella over several other heads.
The kind of cover these figurative um-
brellas provide is not only determined by
belief in God versus unbelief, but also by
faithfulness versus unfaithfulness.

God gave Paul an umbrella of pro-
tection in Acts 27 because of Paul's obedience in ministry. Whether or not the
others realized it, they were gathered under the umbrella and found safety.

You and I are centered on the bow
of the ship when storms come and the
waves crash. May the rest of the crew find
an umbrella of blessing in our midst.

If any of you lacks wisdom, he should ask God, who gives to all generously and without criticizing, and it will be given to him.

James 1:5

One way to have more faith is to ask for it! If you're like me, sometimes we don't need more of anything. We just need the courage to exercise what we already have. Other times we authentically require an increase to do God's will, and He will not refuse it if we ask in Jesus' name.

Jesus will never turn us away when we come to Him with gut-level honesty and request what we lack. Since it is impossible to please God without faith, you and I will constantly have new challenges to believe God. Let's learn to confess our unbelief and ask Christ to empower us to overcome it.

We also speak these things,
not in words taught by human wisdom,
but in those taught by the Spirit.
1 Corinthians 2:13

I've been shocked over the past several years to realize that a few things I was certain were well established in Scripture were actually huge doctrines of man built on single verses. Yes, those Scriptures are still absolutely true, but they don't necessarily warrant building entire, dogmatic belief systems around.

I get a little worried when I can't get Scripture to teach Scripture, when I can get very little applicable permission from the Word. If I can find no other biblical backup for a certain spiritual concept, I tend to think I'm better off accepting by faith what I cannot explain by reason.

That is not how you learned about the
Messiah, assuming you heard Him and were
taught by Him, because the truth is in Jesus.
Ephesians 4:20–21

Some of our beliefs do indeed meet the
test of Scripture, while others need to
be reconsidered. When all is said and
done, we never want our *stand* of faith to
exceed our *walk* of faith. Authentic biblical stands are important, but we need to
see our nouns of belief become present-
active-participle verbs of believing.

Take heart in this assurance: any part
of our long-held belief systems that the
Holy Spirit desires to uproot—beliefs
that are biblically unsupported—will be
replaced with something better and far
more adventurous. Anything not of the
Lord is always the lesser.

I am the LORD, and there is
no other.... I, the LORD, speak
truthfully; I say what is right.
Isaiah 45:18–19

Though many people ask, "Why doesn't
God just prove Himself and His claims?"
He will not allow every shred of doubt
over His existence and creatorship to be
removed. He isn't about to give away all
the answers, because our faith remains
His favorite revelation to a lost world
that He exists.

God allows each of us to take our best
shot at being God. Many intellectuals
proclaim that God has been overruled or
is dead, while they celebrate their heady
victory. But God is secure. He knows who
He is and what He's going to do—in the
course of time.

If I live at the eastern horizon or settle at
the western limits, even there Your hand will
lead me; Your right hand will hold on to me.

Psalm 139:9–10

David, the shepherd-king psalmist, was
an artist. He painted pictures with words.
And he painted one of my favorites in
this passage from Psalm 139.

Just picture a child of God fleeing
from Him to the far side of the sea. Now
imagine God's strong arm stretching
forth from the heavens, His right hand
gripping the prodigal child with such
passion and affection that the veins in
His hand and wrist bulge.

This is what drives our faith. Faith is
complete engagement with God, holding
on to Him and His promises because we
know He's holding on to us.

The Lord God formed the man out
of the dust from the ground and breathed
the breath of life into his nostrils.

Genesis 2:7

You may wonder why God didn't create
our bodies the way He did the other elements of the creation, calling them into
existence from absolutely nothing. He
certainly could have, but He chose not to.
All He had to do was speak.

But I believe God wanted to get His
hands involved. You might say that He
was willing to get His hands dusty. Then
He looked on man and considered him
the finest of all His works.

Remember, our entire purpose for
existence is engagement. Is it little wonder, then, that we were even put together
in an act of engagement?

Which of you, wanting to build a tower,
doesn't first sit down and calculate the cost
to see if he has enough to complete it?

Luke 14:28

Each of us will internally calculate the risks involved in believing God or not believing God. Faith can often seem like risky business.

But actually, we take certain risks whether we choose active faith or not, and we need to weigh them against each other. So ask yourself, "What am I risking if I decide to surrender to a life of present-active-participle believing God? And what am I risking if I don't?"

Be honest with God about this. He knows that each of us is calculating the risk. The most powerful thing we can do is involve Him in the process.

You sent Your good Spirit to
instruct them. You did not withhold
Your manna from their mouths.
Nehemiah 9:20

We will never outgrow our need to be
taught by others who are wiser and more
knowledgeable than we are. The body of
Christ would nearly collapse without the
gift of teaching.

We must be careful, however, not to
fashion our faith secondhand. I still believe much of what I was taught in my
early days of studying solid Bible doctrine, but after years of also seeking God
for myself, I've become convinced that
He is able and willing to do more than
I first imagined. We've got to make sure
that our primary teacher is the Rabboni
Himself, Jesus Christ.

Will not God grant justice to His
elect who cry out to Him day and night?
Will He delay to help them?
Luke 18:7

If a powerful safeguard in Bible study is
to develop our theology primarily on the
Scripture's most repetitive principles, you
will find God's miraculous intervention
among the most repetitive of all. And
since God is never less than who He was
the day He spoke the worlds into orbit,
the challenge placed before us is: "What
would we believe Christ Jesus could do if
all we had was a New Testament?"

We desperately need God to show
His glory, and I believe He's willing. To
use computer terminology, I'm convinced
He's looking for invitations of faith written in bolder fonts!

Do not forget the lives of Your poor people forever. Consider the covenant, for the dark places of the land are full of violence.

Psalm 74:19–20

Destruction and depravity threaten to suffocate our society. Mockers surround us. The enemy seeks to devour us. Church attendance is dropping. Many believers are in bondage. Never before have such haunts of violence filled "the dark places of the land." The last days draw nearer, and many people remain lost.

The world is in desperate need of true spiritual awakening, and believers are in desperate need of a fresh infusion of faith. Yes, we seek God primarily to find Him, not to see Him perform. But may He take His hand from the folds of His garment and show us His glory!

Didn't God choose the poor in this world
to be rich in faith and heirs of the kingdom
He has promised to those who love Him?

James 2:5

God had complete foreknowledge when
He created us. Our infirmities, insecurities, and insufficiencies neither surprised
Him not repulsed Him. They were all
part of the human package. Yet we wonder why He would choose us?

The answer is because He delights
when hearts so prone to wander choose
Him. What would be His greater source
of joy—for perfect people to do perfect
things? Or for pitifully self-centered,
world-centered humans to fight the daily
battle to be God-centered? Beloved, our
victories bring far more delight to God
than our defeats bring disappointment.

By faith Jacob, when he was dying,
blessed each of the sons of Joseph, and, he
worshiped, leaning on the top of his staff.
Hebrews 11:21

Something about picturing the worship
of this old man just before he died is precious. Perhaps the fact that he worshiped
while leaning on his staff indicates he
was too old and feeble to fall prostrate or
even to bow before God.

Close your eyes and imagine the
scene. Also picture his sons and grand-
sons as they watched him. Whether
or not they appreciated it, they were
blessed in more ways than one, weren't
they? That's because few things are more
priceless than a generational heritage of
worship. May we, too, be faithful to pass
one down to those who come behind us.

Avoid irreverent, empty speech,
for this will produce an even greater
measure of godlessness.
2 Timothy 2:16

Few things destroy our witness like rudeness, unkindness, and the like. And I fear that a misinterpreted sense of superiority makes this shortcoming rampant among our religious ranks.

Interestingly, the same Christian who might be appalled over a profane word spoken by someone else might be totally oblivious to the ways she misuses or abuses her own tongue. Perhaps you've heard someone pray at a restaurant, then watched her become so insolent to the waitress that you wanted to crawl under the table. Sins that differ from ours always seem worse.

I will hope continually and will praise You
more and more. My mouth will tell about
Your righteousness . . . all day long.

Psalm 71:14–15

I recently heard a wonderful song con-
fessing that we humans don't have a sea
of forgetfulness. No, you and I don't have
a sea of forgetfulness we can cast things
into. Much of it is all right here.

But the psalmist understood that
the more he focused on his bad or hard
memories, the more downcast he felt. So
he deliberately refocused and reframed
his difficult memories in the goodness
and faithfulness of God.

Short of a lobotomy, we can't throw
away our memories. We have to deal with
them before God. But we need to get our
old pictures in a new frame.

When I saw Him, I fell at His feet
like a dead man. He laid His right hand
on me, and said, "Don't be afraid!"
Revelation 1:17

God is the same yesterday, today, and forever. He is a God so holy, powerful, and present that when He revealed Himself to Ezekiel in the Old Testament and John in the New, both dropped like dead men. He is the magnificent One, full of splendor, beautiful beyond comprehension—the I Am That I Am throughout every generation. Whoever He was, He is. Who He was to them, He is to you.

Start taking Him up on His Godness. When you have no idea what to believe Him for in a given situation, just believe Him to be huge. Come, holy God, and be Thyself.

You are the God of my refuge. Why have
You rejected me? Why must I go about in
sorrow because of the enemy's oppression?

Psalm 43:2

Interestingly, when God withheld His
wonders, the ancient Hebrew people
tended to conclude that something was
wrong.

I am by no means suggesting that
we should assume something is wrong in
our relationship with God if we don't see
miracles. Many variables may be at work
in whether God responds to our prayers,
needs, or desires with an obvious miracle.
I just want to consider that God's wonders were such a part of Israel's history,
the people started asking questions when
they saw little or no divine intervention.
Shouldn't we do the same?

"Why do you ask My name,"
the Angel of the LORD asked him,
"since it is wonderful?"
Judges 13:18

Throughout the annals of history, God presented Himself to His chosen people in many ways and by many titles. Among them were descriptive characteristics like "wonderful" and "marvelous."

I throw around such words fairly frequently, but I love knowing that when I use them to describe God, they take on a more literal meaning. "Wonderful" cannot be disassociated from wonders, nor can "marvelous" be disassociated from marvels. Yes, Jesus is so much more than a miracle worker, but don't miss the fact that God unashamedly associates Himself and His Son with wonders.

To Jesus (mediator of a new covenant),
and to the sprinkled blood, which says
better things than the blood of Abel.
Hebrews 12:24

How I praise God that the sprinkled blood of Christ speaks a better word! I don't want God to simply treat me justly. I've made many mistakes and committed countless sins. I need mercy! How about you? The blood sprinkled from Christ's torn body speaks grace to all who accept the perfect offering by faith.

But though the payment for all our sin has already been made, God still calls His own to obedience. We must not be unwilling to give God what He wants from us the most. Faith means believing that blessing never fails to follow obedience, no matter the sacrifice.

Enoch walked with God 300 years
and fathered sons and daughters. . . .
Enoch walked with God.

Genesis 5:22, 24

When all is said and done, God may have His own personal testimony of all who lived by faith. Don't miss the four-word testimony of one of His saints found in Genesis 5: "Enoch walked with God."

That's all we have to do in order to please God. Walk with Him. He wants our company, and the only way we can walk with Him is to walk by faith and not by sight. The law of Moses did not exist in Enoch's era. He had no rules or regulations. We have no grounds for believing that God appeared to him or spoke aloud from the heavens. In a cold world, Enoch simply had a feverish pursuit of God.

Jesus said to him, "No one who puts
his hand to the plow and looks back
is fit for the kingdom of God."
Luke 9:62

Sometimes we misunderstand where
God has told us to go. Thankfully, He
knows our insecurities and uncertainties.
But very often through Scripture we see
God reconfirm His calling to His child.
If God has granted you several reconfir-
mations of His direction, persevere and
walk with Him there, even if the full purpose of it eludes you.

God does not begrudge our attempts
to make sure we're on the right track—
through the Scripture, through listening,
through the counsel of wise people of
faith. Let's just be sure we don't slip into
practicing unbelief after reconfirmation.

Israel said to Joseph, "Look! I am about to
die, but God will be with you and will bring
you back to the land of your fathers."
Genesis 48:21

Even after this clear pronouncement, the
book of Genesis ends with Joseph dying in Egypt, never making it back to the
land of promise alive. Either someone
was pitching around a false prophecy, or
there's more to blessings than meets the
eye!

Well, God would never affirm faith
in misunderstandings or in misleading
prophecies, so the former premise is out
of the question. Actually, the fulfillment
of this blessing happened just as foretold,
only not in the time frame the hearers
presumed. See, God has a much broader
view when He works in our lives.

I will praise You, because I have been remarkably and wonderfully made. Your works
are wonderful, and I know this very well.

Psalm 139:14

Though he lived several thousand years
before Charles Darwin, a simple shepherd's inspired appreciation for the wonders of human existence far surpassed
the human hypotheses of an acclaimed
scientist who convinced much of the
world that he had the answers.

For example, while Darwin sat at his
desk and reduced all creation to simple
blobs of protoplasm, the outstretched
DNA in his body could have reached
back and forth to the sun about fifty
times. Charles Darwin was fearfully and
wonderfully made. He just never knew it.
So are you, Dear One.

DECEMBER

The LORD said to Abram: "Go out from
your land, your relatives, and your father's
house to the land that I will show you."

Genesis 12:1

I love the way the King James Version
renders the first part of this command
from Genesis 12:1—"Get thee out of thy
country." Very few of us took our first
leaps of faith without hearing God say
into our spiritual ears, "Get thee out of
thy comfort zone."

Let's put it another way: if we were
already where we're going, for all practical earthly purposes we'd be dead. We can
rest assured that what God has for us—
even in our earthly future—is not identi-
cal to our present. Whether we like it or
not, a fair amount of going is involved in
following.

We want each of you to
demonstrate the same diligence for
the final realization of your hope.
Hebrews 6:11

One of Abraham's monumental tests remains a painstaking challenge for each of us today. Between "go" and "receive" is more often than not the faith test of time. Allow me to rename this condition the Later Syndrome. Few of us will miss it, because it's too important.

Would it help to know that Christ also experienced the test of time? He didn't perform His first miracle until He was thirty years old. If we didn't know better, we might think God was running a little late, considering Jesus had only three years remaining in His earthly ministry. Nope. He was right on time.

The one who plants and the one who
waters are equal, and each will receive his
own reward according to his own labor.

1 Corinthians 3:8

Our lives build on the faithfulness of the
believing generation before us, and those
after us will build on ours. Our ego says,
"If I don't do the planting, sowing, growing, and harvesting, none of it will get
done." We're mistaken. As much as we'd
like to think otherwise, we have just one
little piece, and our faithfulness with it is
paramount.

God uses time to prepare us to build
with what we're given. He calls us to make
contributions of quality, not just quantity.
We waste time when our impatience for
earthly inheritance keeps us from knowing what to do with it.

"If I want him to remain until I come,"
Jesus answered, "what is that to you?
As for you, follow Me."
John 21:22

One of our challenges is watching others who seem to be operating effectively in their Promised Land, while we still feel like aliens in tents, wondering whether we misunderstood.

To add insult to injury, some of these people we're watching may be younger than we are! Have you ever found this frustrating?

But not only is comparison a waste of time, it can also be deadly. If we're not careful, we can allow resentment to kill our opportunity to grow. God reserves the right to handle us as individually as the prints He stamped on our fingertips.

"Don't You have an answer to what these men are testifying against You?" But He kept silent and did not answer anything.

Mark 14:60–61

Trusting in the sovereign plan of God even necessitated that Christ not always act, though He certainly had the ability to. What might have happened if He had always exercised His power rather than trusting God and refusing to be goaded into action?

If we've walked with God for very long at all, we've each faced times when faith required us not to act, even though everything within us was wanting to take action. Even the most action-oriented among us must learn to sit on our hands when challenged to do things in our own power, outside of God's timetable.

Jesus responded to them,
"My Father is still working,
and I am working also."
John 5:17

If you belong to Christ, you need to know that He and His Father are not only at work continually in the universe and among believers as a whole. They are also and always at work in you through the third member of the Trinity.

What you and I desperately need is keener spiritual vision to behold some of their activity and to sense their presence. What have we got to lose besides a load of defeat and doubt?

If God said it, I want to believe it. If God gives it, I want to receive it. If God shows it, I want to perceive it. If Satan stole it, I want to retrieve it.

They saw a large crowd around them and scribes disputing with them. . . . He asked, "What are you arguing with them about?"

Mark 9:14, 16

Mark 9 records a very interesting interchange between Christ and His disciples after some of them were unable to cast a demon from a tormented child. I am convinced that the argument they had with some of the educated, dignified teachers of the law diminished their faith so drastically, they were unable to do one of the very things they had been empowered by Christ to do.

If you want to be full of faith, don't argue with a legalist! Love them. Serve side-by-side with them if God wills. Don't judge them. But understand that unbelief is highly contagious.

I am putting a stone in Zion to stumble over, and a rock to trip over, yet the one who believes on Him will not be put to shame.

Romans 9:33

I'll show you what I've learned to assume when a mountain won't budge. When Jesus said in Matthew 17:20 that we could tell mountains to move, He didn't generalize His illustration with "any" mountain. He specifically said we could speak to "this" mountain. To what mountain did He refer? He and the disciples had just come down from the mountain of His transfiguration.

So if you have the faith in God to tell a mountain to move—and it won't—assume that Christ wants you to climb it instead and see Him transfigured. Either way, the mountain is under your feet.

For this I suffer, to the point
of being bound like a criminal;
but God's message is not bound.

2 Timothy 2:9

Paul believed what Christ believed. It's what made him who he was. He did not make *it*—it was making *him.* It was the very truth of God and not the invention of any human. No whip could beat it out of him. From his last imprisonment he wrote that although he was chained, God's Word was not chained.

Indeed! God sends forth His Word, and it never returns void, unchaining the soul of every person who has the courage to believe it. May we, then, commission each other to spend our lives devouring His Word. Breathe it. Speak it. Live it. Love it. And brace yourself for it.

And they will be called
righteous trees, planted by
the LORD, to glorify Him.
Isaiah 61:3

We are no longer under the law and authority of our pasts, but we are free to use them as they lend expression to our faith in Jesus. As much as you might not want to hear this, you couldn't become the servant God is calling you to be without the threads of your past being knitted into the Technicolor fabric of your future.

God is far too practical to allow your heritage to have absolutely nothing to do with your future, I am convinced this is true in my own life. God is never more glorified than when He brings an oak of righteousness out of what was once so damaged a root.

He will not forget your work and the love
you showed for His name when you served
the saints—and you continue to serve them.

Hebrews 6:10

Believing in Christ and believing Christ
can be two very different things. We all
begin with the former, but we certainly
don't want to end there! We want to keep
believing what Jesus says about Himself
and His Father—and about us—until we
see Him face to face.

Think of the roll call of the faithful
in Hebrews 11. As eternally vital as it is,
none of these were commended for the
initial faith that enabled them to enter a
relationship with God. They were commended for ongoing acts of believing at
times when their physical eyes could not
see what God had promised them.

He answered, "Whether or not He's a
sinner, I don't know. One thing I do know:
I was blind, and now I can see!"

John 9:25

Who is your Jesus? Who do you believe
Jesus to be with your life? In reality, what
we believe is measured by what we live,
not by what we say. If your life were a
Gospel like those in the Bible, who could
people believe your Jesus to be?

Think specifically and concretely.
Based on your life, might people believe
Jesus to be a Redeemer because He has
obviously redeemed your life from a pit?
Or a Healer because He has healed you
from a certain disease? Questions like
these help us see our progress in the faith,
giving us reason for rejoicing and helping
us see where He wants us to go.

They want to be teachers of the law,
although they don't understand what they
are saying or what they are insisting on.

1 Timothy 1:7

I derived most of my early impressions
about Jesus based not so much on what I
learned at church but what I *saw* at church.
I certainly believed Jesus saves. But I believed Him for little more because I saw
evidence of little more. Perhaps, like me,
you have derived a staggering amount of
your impressions of Christ from vastly in-
complete if not totally unreliable sources,
as sweet and respectable as they may be.

The few marvelous exceptions have
marked me forever, but I wonder why so
many believers believe so little of Jesus.
Either He no longer does what the Bible
says, or we don't give Him the chance.

God is able to make every grace overflow
to you, so that in every way, always having
everything you need, you may excel.
2 Corinthians 9:8

The only excuse for even a single ounce
of victory in my life is the supernatural
delivering power of Jesus Christ. I was in
the clutches of a real, live devil, living in a
perpetual cycle of defeat. Only a miracle-
working God could have set me free, then
dared to use me.

You may remark, "That's not a real
miracle!" but Scripture suggests that no
greater work exists. The most profound
miracles of God will always be those
within the hearts and souls of people.
Moving a mountain is nothing compared
to changing a selfish, destructive human
heart into something He can use.

Then Jesus said to him,
"'If You can?' Everything is possible
to the one who believes."
Mark 9:23

Through His work on the cross and His plan before the foundation of the world, Christ has already accomplished so much for your life in heaven. But if His work is going to be accomplished here on earth where your feet hit the hot pavement, you need to start believing Him. Now!

When we received Christ as Savior, it was like a pipe of power connecting our lives to God's throne. Unbelief clogs the pipe, but the act of believing clears the way for the inconceivable. If we don't see miracles, let it be because He showed His glory another way, not because we believed Him for so pitifully little.

He has satisfied the
thirsty and filled the hungry
with good things.
Psalm 107:9

When my daughter Melissa was a toddler, she was never satisfied with just a little of anything. Every time I offered her a treat, she'd cup her plump little hand, thrust it forward, and say, "Can me have a bunch of it?" The way she saw life, why bother with a little if you could have a big bunch of it? Indeed!

How tragic for us to continue with pangs of emptiness. What a waste! Christ came to bring us a bunch of it! So stop feeling guilty because you crave lots of joy in life. You were made for joy! You are a jar of clay waiting to be filled. Let's toast to a life overflowing with new wine!

Love the Lord your God with all
your heart, with all your soul, with all
your mind, and with all your strength.

Mark 12:30

I am convinced that virtually everything
in an individual believer's life hinges on
his or her deliberate belief and active acceptance of the lavish, unconditional love
of God. I'm not sure we can be reminded
too often of God's absolute priorities for
our lives.

No matter how different our gifts,
personalities, denominations, or styles of
worship, God's chief priority for each one
of us is that we love Him with everything
in us. But like two chambers in one heart,
the lifeblood of His first priority cannot
flow apart from the second: that we love
others as ourselves.

All the LORD's ways show
faithful love and truth to those who
keep His covenant and decrees.
Psalm 25:10

One of the biggest hang-ups many people
have in loving God and others lavishly is
a distrust or unwilling acceptance of the
immutable fact of God's love. Everything
begins there.

How can we get on with loving God
and loving others? We can consider all
God has said and done to prove His love
to us through His Word and His Son.
Then we can confess the sin of unbelief
and choose to act upon what God has
said and done regardless of the ebb and
flow of our emotions.

If we would but practice this daily,
how our lives would change!

Having been justified by
His grace, we may become heirs
with the hope of eternal life.

Titus 3:7

Daily we say all kinds of things about ourselves. Sometimes what we say about ourselves is not necessarily accurate, but it's what we believe.

Trust me, I know about this one. I lived much of my life with a highly inaccurate estimation of who I wasn't and who I was. As a young person, I swung dizzily between feelings of "I am a victim and I'm not as good as anybody else" to "I'm no one's victim and I'm going to be *better* than everyone else." Believing and living a lie is so exhausting. What finally got me off the swing? Learning to see myself in relationship to Jesus Christ.

"Master," Simon replied, "we've worked hard
all night long and caught nothing! But at
Your word, I'll let down the nets."

Luke 5:5

Peter and his companions had worked
hard. Day in and day out. Then one day
Jesus walked up and everything changed.

Isn't that exactly like Him? Jesus
walks right up, catches us in the act of being—again today—exactly who we were
yesterday, and offers to turn our routine
into adventure. Have you allowed Christ
to do that for you?

If you're bored with life and stuck in
a rut of routine, you may have believed in
Christ, but you may not yet have agreed
to follow Him. Christ is a lot of things,
but boring? Not on your life! Life with
Him is a great adventure.

I also saw the Holy City, new Jerusalem,
coming down out of heaven from God, prepared like a bride adorned for her husband.
Revelation 21:2

I believe heaven will be far more creative
than most believers seem to picture it.
Surely a God who created this world with
all its magnificence, diversity, and experience does not have an eternal home that
is like a one-act play. I hardly think so.

Nor can I buy that we'll always be
in one huge corporate gathering. How
in the world could private encounters
happen with millions of the redeemed in
heaven?

The way I see it, that's one reason
we have eternity. Plenty of time for each
of us to have Jesus all to ourselves. Oh, I
think we have lots of surprises in store.

When the disciples
heard it, they fell facedown
and were terrified.
Matthew 17:6

All three synoptic Gospels record the transfiguration, but only Matthew's account supplies the detail that the three disciples fell facedown to the ground.

I am convinced that the people of God miss many appropriate opportunities to fall facedown to the ground, not in an emotional frenzy but in complete awe of God.

Oftentimes we don't have a clue who we're dealing with. I believe one of Jesus' chief reasons for transfiguring Himself before the three disciples was to say, "I am not like you. This is just a glimpse of who I am."

Abba, Father! All things are possible for You.
Take this cup away from Me. Nevertheless,
not what I will, but what You will.

Mark 14:36

Sometimes obeying God in a matter will
be the hardest thing we've ever done in
our lives. We are not wrong to feel. We
are only wrong to disobey.

Hash it out with God. Ask for the cup
to be removed. But resolve to do His will,
no matter what. Glory is at stake. That's
why Jesus drew the three disciples close
enough to see. To teach them to pray—
not to sleep—in their anguish.

This time they slept. They had little
power to do otherwise. But a time would
come when each would rise from his own
Gethsemane and bear his cross. Salvation
always necessitates a cross.

The angel said to them, "Don't be afraid,
for look, I proclaim to you good news of
great joy that will be for all the people."
Luke 2:10

I am convinced God wants us to get involved in our Scripture reading. Using
our imaginations and picturing the events
as eyewitnesses can make black ink on a
white page spring into living color.

No matter how the glory of God
appeared, it scared the shepherds half
to death. The words of the angel are so
reminiscent of Jesus. He often told those
nearly slain by His glory not to be afraid.

Oh, how I love Him! The untouch-
able Hand of God reaching down to
touch the fallen hand of man. May we,
like the shepherds, waste no time em-
bracing the news.

While they were there, the time
came for her to give birth. Then she
gave birth to her firstborn Son.
Luke 2:6–7

In the Jewish calendar, the fourteenth
day of the first month is called the day
of conception. If our God of perfect
planning and gloriously significant order happened to overshadow Mary on
the fourteenth day of the first month of
His calendar, our Savior would have been
born toward the end of our December.

We have absolutely no way of knowing whether or not He did, but I would
not be the least bit surprised for God to
have sparked His Son's human life on one
Passover and ended it on another. Until a
further "Hear ye! Hear ye!" from heaven,
December 25 works fine for me.

He named it Ebenezer,
explaining, "The LORD has
helped us to this point."
1 Samuel 7:12

Ebenezer means "stone of help," like the
one Samuel set up to memorialize the
great victory that was won after Israel's
repentance from years of idolatry. As we
walk out the remainder of our time line of
faith, let's keep memorializing God's obvious interventions through such stones
of remembrance. And let's keep walking
by faith with an "Ebenezer" stone in our
hand until we see the next astonishing
evidence of His promises.

Ebenezer stones constantly remind
us that with God's help we've made it "up
to this point." And we can be sure we'll
make it some more.

There has been no day like it before or since, when the LORD listened to the voice of a man, because the LORD fought for Israel.

Joshua 10:14

As badly as the Israelites smelled after their victory at Gibeon—the time when the Lord caused the sun to stand still in the sky for a full day—not one soldier in Joshua's army was heard saying, "I wish I'd stayed home. I may never get the stains out of this robe or the broken strap fixed on my sandal."

No, their grandchildren sat spellbound at each retelling. There had never been a day like it, and they wouldn't have missed it for the world. Sometimes God requires much of us so we can experience the unmatched exhilaration of partnering in divine triumph.

Give glory to the LORD your God
before He brings darkness, before your feet
stumble on the mountains at dusk.
Jeremiah 13:16

I remember the day when rising flood-waters came within an inch of our back door. My normally soft-spoken husband raised his right hand and said, "Stretch forth Your mighty hand, O God, and recede the waters." Instantly, the torrent turned to sprinkles. The rain stopped.

I'm convinced that if I had asked the same thing, God probably wouldn't have done it . . . or at least not so dramatically. My man needed to know that God is as willing to work in his life as his wife's.

Stop looking at others as if they are so much more spiritual than you and just start believing God!

Don't worry about tomorrow,
because tomorrow will worry about itself.
Each day has enough trouble of its own.
Matthew 6:34

I can remember in the early days of getting through the withdrawal of addictive sin, I'd seek God in the morning, then live on His sufficiency until noon. Then until dinner. Then until bedtime. Then the worst time of all: the black of the long night. I begged God to help me.

One day turned into two. Two days turned into seven. Weeks into months. Months into one year. Then two. Then three. Then four. Then ten.

That's how we did it. And we are making it, God and I, one day at a time. If you tumble into unbelief, stand back to your feet . . . and just start walking again.

They did not receive what
was promised, since God had
provided something better for us.
Hebrews 11:39–40

Hebrews 11 is commonly called the hall
of faith. It is God's testimony of flesh-
and-blood faithfulness. But while all of
those mentioned here lived lives of faith
and gained the evidence of many promises, none received every promise in their
earthly lifetime. Verse 40 says, "They
would not be made perfect without us."

Dear One, you are the continuance
of Hebrews 11. It concludes with verse
40, but I think God might have each of
us see ourselves as Hebrews 11:41. When
He pens the final dot on our earthly time
lines, His lasting testimony of our lives
will be what we did . . . by faith.

We ask and encourage you in the Lord Jesus,
that as you have received from us how you
must walk and please God, do so even more.
1 Thessalonians 4:1

I am praying with all my heart that this won't have been just another book. Believing God isn't a book or a Bible study. It's a lifestyle. And I'm praying that the faith adventure suggested in these pages has only begun for you now that you've reached the end of the year.

Nothing is like experiencing the affirming, undeniable nod of God. So I'm praying that He will do something obvious to show you that you're on the right track—so that when seasons come with fewer evidences, you'll have the unwavering assurance that God is believable. Go into this new year believing God!